The Cultural Toolbox

The Cultural Toolbox

Traditional Ojibwe Living in the Modern World

Anton Treuer

mnhspress.org

The Minnesota Historical Society Press is a member of the Association of University Presses.

Manufactured in the United States of America

10 9 8 7 6 5 4 3 2

∞ The paper used in this publication meets the minimum requirements of the American National Standard for Information Sciences—Permanence for Printed Library Materials, ANSI Z39.48-1984.

International Standard Book Number
ISBN: 978-1-68134-214-6 (paper)
ISBN: 978-1-68134-215-3 (e-book)

Library of Congress Control Number: 2021941313

This and other Minnesota Historical Society Press books are available from popular e-book vendors.

For my dauntless product and purveyor of the cultural toolbox,
Chi-ogimaa-binesiikwe (Big Boss Eagle Woman),
my daughter Luella Treuer

Contents

The Cultural Toolbox

INTRODUCTION
Ojibwe Seasons

MY HANDS WERE TREMBLING slightly as I grasped the first pouch of tobacco. I was only twenty-seven years old. I was young and strong, so it was weird to see my hands shake.

The dance hall at Round Lake, on the St. Croix Reservation in Wisconsin, was a tiny building with white-painted walls that had long ago acquired a weathered grayish color from years of steady use—muddy kid fingerprints that had never quite wiped fully clean, a film of tobacco smoke from numerous social and ceremonial smokings. It would be hard to describe the place as regal to an outsider, but that's what it was to me.

There were around two hundred people packed in that little building, sitting side by side, three rows deep, around the edges of the grayish walls. They were laughing and eagerly visiting with one another. Kids were all over the place, too, some milling around the edges near their parents and grandparents, but mostly sent outside to play in the late summer sun so they wouldn't disturb the doings inside. Many of the attendees were fluent Ojibwe speakers, singers, and tribal culture carriers of every kind. There were at least twenty ceremonial drum chiefs present. They were gathering for a drum ceremony, as they did in Round Lake a dozen times a year. I admired them. The St. Croix Ojibwe were the descendants of those who had refused to leave their ancestral homes along the Minnesota-Wisconsin border and relocate to Lac Courte Oreilles and other Ojibwe reservations in the late 1800s. They just stayed where they had always lived as their lands filled up with white settlers. Their rights to stay there weren't even validated until after the Indian Reorganization Act of 1934, within the living memories of many of the elders in attendance. They were so tenacious. And they knew so much.

I had been a longtime apprentice to Archie Mosay, one of the great spiritual leaders from the area. He was born in a wigwam in 1901, raised speaking Ojibwe only. He didn't even get the name Archie until he was a teenager, soon after the first time he met a white man—a local farmer who he ended up working for. The farmer said he'd never be able to pronounce the name Niibaa-giizhig (Evening Sky), so he named him Archie, and it stuck. Archie's Ojibwe namesakes were US Civil War veterans. He was in his thirties when he first met a Black man and first saw a car. He was too old to serve in World War II. And I had stumbled into a life-altering journey with him in 1991, when he was already ninety years old. I pestered that old man for years, living on his couch at times, driving him to funerals, carrying his pipe and drum to various ceremonies. I was just excited to be there and see into the Ojibwe culture—my culture—in a way that few Ojibwe are privileged to see.

Sitting with Archie Mosay at the ceremonial grounds in Balsam Lake, Wisconsin.
Misty Mosay

People came from all over Wisconsin and Minnesota to see Archie. They wanted Indian names. They needed him to officiate funerals for their loved ones. They wanted medicine, healing, initiation into our sacred society. And they came to the drum ceremonies there, too, to honor the drums, but also to hear him sing (which he did even in his nineties) and listen to him speak for the feasts and bundles. The old man had a natural second-bass voice. It was deep, resonant, and amazingly loud. It was a special experience just to hear him.

But something was different in 1997. Archie had died the year before. They were breaking a bundle—a special way to honor the dead and bring the bereaved relatives out of mourning. Lots of people wanted to be there, to honor Archie. And they all wondered who would be speaking. The room was full of competent speakers, deeply knowledgeable about the drums, fluent in our language. But they had always deferred to Archie. It would be novel and strange to hear someone else talk for the feast.

Betsy Schultz was one of Archie's children. She was in her seventies now. She had lupus and got around in a wheelchair, using a cane to stand when she needed to. She shook that cane at her grandkids with some regularity, too. But with me, she had always been super sweet. She would kiss me on both cheeks every time we met and hug me close. I always remember the softness of her skin and her disposition toward me—it stood in contrast to her dark shaded glasses, which framed the perfect "mean Indian look" she used when she was getting her grandkids in line, which was a permanent occupation for her.

At the drum ceremonies, the main feast is set on tables—maybe a hundred bowls of venison, pork chops, wild rice hotdish, potato salad, beans, boiled eggs, and frybread. People who wanted to make special requests of the drum brought additional bowls of food and tobacco, and they asked for special prayers—to help a sick

Betsy Schultz holding my daughter Madeline. *Anton Treuer*

relative, to watch over a relative serving as a soldier overseas, or to remember a relative who had passed away and send food to them in the spirit world.

Betsy was only a foot away, but she was staring at me. For the first time, she was looking at me the way she looked at her grandkids—stern, serious, and like she was ready to tune me up with her cane. "You're talking today," she told me. "You followed my dad around these past years, and now I'm going to hear what you learned." There were thirteen bowls on the ground, each for a different request from a different person. Betsy placed the first pouch of tobacco in my hand. "That's for my dad's spirit bowl." My hand shook. Then she lined up all the other people and had each tell me their Indian name and what their bowl was for. I had pouches of tobacco between all my fingers on both my left and right hands and five more in my palms. Betsy leaned closer. "My dad never forgot what a bowl was for. And never forgot an Indian name. I'll be listening."

I felt very young as I stood up. Nobody could replace Archie, though I knew someone had to succeed him. And his kids wanted me to be the voice that followed his. The audience was older and more knowledgeable than me, but I had to honor the request. I'm a baritone, not a bass, and I was young, not old. All Ojibwe ceremonies are conducted exclusively in Ojibwe. I am a second-language learner, not a first speaker, and I had nowhere near the eloquence of Archie. But I gave the effort everything I had. When I finished the main talk and ran through all of the special requests, I placed the tobacco pouches by the drum and dared a glance back at Betsy. She gave me a single, slow, affirmative nod. Then she shook her cane at her grandkids to go eat out of the bowls.

I knew something had happened for me then. There was no going back. I often speak at ceremonial drums now—prayers, special requests, and the legend of the drums. I sing often, too, and there is a lot of complicated music on the drums. I officiate at funerals. I give Indian names. I travel a lot, and people come to see me. I love being in the service of others and the spirits that watch over us all.

But it wasn't always this way. My father, Robert Treuer, wasn't even Native. He was an Austrian Jewish immigrant and a Holocaust survivor. My mother, Margaret Treuer, was Ojibwe and grew up in the village of Bena on the Leech Lake Reservation in northern Minnesota. But her mom was taken to residential boarding school, where she lost her language and picked up Catholicism. As an adult, my mom sought to reclaim her Ojibwe religion and ways, but it was a relearning effort for her. I grew up in Bemidji, a town on the edge of the Leech Lake Reservation, with lots of Natives and many more whites. Some parts of the Ojibwe cultural toolbox were familiar to me—making maple syrup in the spring, hunting rabbits, grouse, and deer, going to powwows and sweat lodge ceremonies. But other things were completely unfamiliar until I got older, like drum ceremony and medicine dance. These gatherings are our primary religious societies. We don't advertise them in a paper, as we often do for powwows. Finding out about those ceremonies and where they take place is difficult if you're not from a family that regularly participates. When I finished high school, I was more interested in running away from Ojibwe country than learning more about it. I ended up going to Princeton University for my undergraduate degree. But by the end of college, I was hungry for my culture. That's how I found Archie.

Learning one's culture should not be hard, but for an Indigenous person, it often is. The Ojibwe are an especially large group. There are around 250,000 Ojibwe in the United States alone, spread across Michigan, Wisconsin, Minnesota, North Dakota, and a mixed Ojibwe-Cree reservation in Montana. And we are in Canada, too, in 141 First Nations communities from Quebec to Saskatchewan. In former times, all of those communities had many spiritual leaders, keepers of medicine, knowledgeable orators and singers, ceremonial drum keepers, funeral officiants, and medicine dance practitioners. When I wanted to go through the medicine dance, there were only seven active medicine dance lodges in all of the United States and Canada. Archie was chief for one of them, and he was the oldest and most famous of them all. So, I took a 245-mile drive to look for Archie.

This was before the age of cell phones. When I arrived in his hometown of Balsam Lake, Wisconsin, I started looking up Mosays in the phone book at a coin-operated pay phone. The first one I spoke to was his son Dan, who was skeptical and protective but eventually told me how to find his dad. I was a little surprised when I walked in the door to Archie's tiny but modern house to see him sitting in an armchair watching WWF SummerSlam professional wrestling on the television and laughing loudly. He gave me a long look, then shut off the TV and said, "I've been waiting for you." This confused me, but he soon explained that he'd had a dream that someone was coming to see him and that I looked like the person from his dream. He opened up to me, and I eagerly devoured every bit of guidance and instruction that he threw my way. In a fairly short time, I was initiated into the medicine dance and began to help Archie at ceremonies in many different ways.

Mine was a rare and privileged position, to see many sides to his spiritual work and service. I had an immersive experience in our language and culture. I quickly abandoned my previous dreams of being a lawyer or politician. I wanted to be a full-time Ojibwe person—I had no interest in walking in two worlds. The Ojibwe world was calling me, and the white one lost all appeal. My parents refused to keep their Ivy League–educated son as a dependent, so I ran out of money and had to get a job. I worked as a student support counselor at Bemidji State University for a while, splitting time between my childhood home and Archie's. Eventually I went to graduate school. I'm now a professor of the Ojibwe language at Bemidji State University. But my real education didn't take place in the hallowed halls of academia; it happened in a wigwam sitting next to that old man who never finished the second grade. Over a period of several years, I was given a pipe, I went fasting, and I was seated on a number of ceremonial big drums as a speaker and a singer. Today I follow the cultural roads that Archie blazed throughout his life, although I never do the work as proficiently as he did.

As I have aged, and raised children, and more recently become a grandparent, I've come to realize how special my experience with Archie was. There are literally hundreds of thousands of Ojibwe people, and many are hungry for a cultural experience like the one I had. For generations, Ojibwe language and culture have been under assault through boarding schools and a host of other pernicious assimilation policies. Colonization is the effort to use one culture and language to supplant others. Colonization is erasure, and it creates terrible wounds and trauma. And that's exactly what the Ojibwe and other Indigenous people have been subjected to for generations. The critical effort is not simply to identify colonization and what it did to us, but to stop the damage and start the healing. Decolonization can mean many things, but learning one's heritage culture is a powerful process, and it is very healing. Many of us want our children to get Native names, know their clans, and be familiar with the rich cultural patrimony of our people. But that beautiful culture seems just out of reach for far too many people. The Ojibwe culture is under stress right now. The hunger is there, but access to reliable, approachable, usable cultural information and experience is elusive for many. I want to change that.

I am frequently in conversation with other Ojibwe culture carriers, and we all feel overwhelmed by the demand for our services as funeral officiants, name givers, and practitioners of our sacred ceremonies. Demand for cultural knowledge has outpaced access to language and culture, and there aren't enough of us to do all the work. Many people are working to change this. While I know I am working as *hard* as I can, I have been asking myself whether I have been working as *smart* as I can. That is why I am writing this book.

A book is a powerful way to share information with more people more quickly. It can preserve and strengthen the teaching of our culture. Some parts of our culture can be shared in a book, but some parts of our culture cannot. The Ojibwe culture is alive. It has many practitioners, and it has rules. I'm not writing this for posterity. I am writing this to catalyze the stabilization and growth of our living culture, so I need you to understand what I can and cannot write about. Some kinds of cultural information do not belong in a book; this sometimes frustrates those who are eager to learn more about the Ojibwe culture. But my reasons for saying this are both practical and spiritual. One of the keys to my own success at cultural learning is that I not simply had access to the words Archie had to say but spent so much time listening to him say the words over and over again. There is no shortcut to learning a culture. Those who want to carry it have to live it and put in the time. We have to go to our elders with our tobacco rather than walk around them and get our information solely from a book. This is a practical perspective about the cultural learning process.

There is a spiritual dimension to this as well. When we do our most sacred ceremonies, we give legends and songs as part of those ceremonies. But we do not give only the intellectual part of story and song—we also give the spiritual part of story and song. If I give someone a song, I am literally pulling that song out of my soul and putting it into theirs. If we skip the soul-to-soul transmission, we short-circuit its spiritual essence and power. This is why the many anthropologists who have tried to pull together cultural information on the Ojibwe do very little to help us keep our culture alive. If I learn a song from a Frances Densmore wax cylinder recording, I might learn the musicology and words to that song, but I cannot acquire, through a recording, either the right to use that song or the spiritual empowerment of that song. That spiritual potency is only conferred when cultural information is transmitted in its true cultural environment and through our Ojibwe process. It's like the words to a song and its musical notes together constitute a cup that holds the song's spirit. What use is the cup without its contents? Nobody can make a book about the Ojibwe culture that keeps the Ojibwe culture alive, and an attempt at doing so might even undermine our people's reliance on the time-tested protocols for acquiring sacred information.

In addition to that, since I am someone who carries rare cultural information and lives a life in the service of our people, it is important to me to keep our sacred information in our sacred spaces. I have to protect the sanctity of our ceremonial process. This book will not be violating any taboos or weakening that process and protocol. This is not a book about the medicine dance, shake tent, drum ceremony, or traditional Ojibwe funeral. This isn't a bible on Ojibwe ways.

However, while I will not be trespassing on our long-standing taboos about what can be shared in book form or in mixed company, there are many dimensions of Ojibwe culture beyond "how to do a ceremony" that are safe and fine to share in a format like this. It amazes me to see not what we have lost but what we still have. In spite of everything we have endured, my people still have a rich, deep, beautiful culture. I am writing this book first of all to help Ojibwe people who are hungry for their own culture and find it difficult to access. For those who are interested in learning what the Ojibwe cultural toolbox can show them about navigating the birth of a child, Ojibwe harvest practices, relationships with the natural world, and many other things, this book should be a helpful resource.

This book also offers non-Ojibwe people a chance to see and appreciate authentic cultural information about the first people of the land without appropriating any of it. In this day and age, cultural misunderstandings and absent narratives drive damaging wedges between groups. It is my hope that the content of this book can generate genuine understanding and build bridges to help us traverse difficult times and more effectively engineer healthy connection and inclusivity.

Some of our cultural practices are place based. We harvest wild rice, for example, only where the wild rice grows. I've been both lucky and intentional about where I live—in the heart of Ojibwe country on private land with an abundance of resources that make some of our cultural practices both natural and easier to do. Not everyone has this, which can be an extra barrier for those who are getting started but live in urban areas or away from some of these place-based activities. I offer guidance as best I can. The natural world is all around us, even in cities. I once picked medicine at a park in the heart of St. Paul. And even urban folks can often find ways to take a trip and forage for mushrooms—harvesting for private use is legal in state parks. Mille Lacs is less than a two-hour drive from Minneapolis, and the St. Croix Reservation is only an hour away. Walpole Island First Nation is just an hour's drive from Detroit. Centers of cultural practice are often much closer than people think, and getting there is worth the effort. Even more importantly, while place-based cultural practices require us to get to certain places, we can also cultivate our own cultural practices. Connection and culture live *inside* of us. Having a rich cultural life is not just about looking out and looking for; it is about looking within. We can do that wherever we live. The awakening is healing and empowering.

Sharing the Ojibwe culture can be beautiful, but it can also be a tricky enterprise. The reason is simple: there is no such thing as *the* Ojibwe culture. The Ojibwe are a very large group and have many different cultures, which vary tremendously by geography. What it means to be Ojibwe at Bear Island, Ontario, on the Quebec border, is very different from what it means at Turtle Mountain, North Dakota. What people cook, how they organize their government, how they greet each other in those places is not the same. For starters, wild rice doesn't even grow in either place! But it's a staple food and defining feature of Ojibwe culture at Lac Courte Oreilles, Wisconsin. Ojibwe cultures also change over time. How people fished by light at night in 1600 is very different from how people do that now. Even in the same community at the same point in time, you will see a great deal of variation in cultural practices and faith traditions. My mother's home village of Bena has people who follow traditional Ojibwe religious beliefs and funeral practices, but it also has Catholics, Episcopalians, and agnostics.

This book does not try to cover all of the hundreds of different Ojibwe cultures. I am simply going to share *my* Ojibwe culture. My Ojibwe culture is not new; I learned from Archie Mosay and many other great Ojibwe culture carriers. They knew their stuff, but my Ojibwe culture is not "the way," "the only way," "the best way," or a way that should be used to evaluate anyone else's way. I think Archie's way was different from that of his grandfather because they lived in different times. The image of Archie sitting in a chair watching professional wrestling on a television set would have seemed like a totally different culture to his grandfather. So, my Ojibwe culture is informed by the Ojibwe cultures of my ancestors, but it is not the same as the culture of my ancestors. Likewise, my Ojibwe culture is something I actively teach to my nine children and growing number of grandchildren, but their Ojibwe culture will necessarily diverge from mine to accommodate the technology changes and climate changes and other changes certain to happen in their lifetimes. Who knows? Maybe they'll do naming ceremonies by hologram in the future. Maybe wild rice won't grow on planet earth anymore. But there can still be Ojibwe cultures. Cultures are always changing, shifting, evolving. My culture is not new, and it is not new age. I am not making this up. But this isn't exactly what people did hundreds of years ago. It's traditional Ojibwe living in the modern world.

The Ojibwe often use the four seasons as a metaphor for life. There are four seasons in a year—spring, summer, fall, and winter. These seasons are also represented in the Ojibwe cosmos as the four cardinal points on the compass. East is spring, where the sun rises and the cycle of seasons begins. It's symbolic of birth and new life, and it corresponds with the first of four major phases of life: birth and infancy. South is summer. The sun tracks from east to west across the southern half of the sky. Summer symbolizes warmth, strength, youth, and vibrancy. In the cycle of life, this represents young people. West is autumn. This is the season when game is fat and plentiful and wild rice and other crops are harvested. It's symbolic of adulthood, parenting, and maturity. North is winter. The days are shorter, covered in a blanket of white snow. But this is the season of wisdom and heightened knowledge, when stories are told. It's represented by elderhood in the cycle of life. This metaphor is applied to the cycle of life and all things in it, even the cycles of marriage.

I've organized this book with that metaphor in mind. There are four main sections, each devoted to one of these phases of life and the cultural practices associated with it. This is my Ojibwe culture, and there is no way to separate the culture from its practitioners, so in the pages to come you'll get to know me and my family as well as what we do through the seasons each year. Gimiigwechiwi'in—thank you for taking a journey into my world. Welcome.

SPRING
New Life

OUR NINTH AND FINAL CHILD was on her way in September 2011. My wife, Blair, was already dilating, and everything in her body said this would be a quick labor and relatively easy birth. I thought I was a professional at the dad role by now. I had an Ojibwe-birthing go bag with everything I needed for the baby's first bath and for bringing the placenta home to bury by a maple tree. I activated a phone tree we'd set up, so babysitters rushed to the house and Blair's mom and sister converged on the hospital in minutes. I was managing everything like an experienced air traffic controller on Thanksgiving Day. And nothing went the way I expected. There were complications. Blair needed a cesarean section. Baby was

Luella, spearfishing. ***Anton Treuer***

breathing fine, but jaundiced, slow to cry or react to stimuli from the nurses, and seemingly uninterested in nursing.

Blair and I called one of my trusted mentors, Anna Gibbs. Anna was a remarkable woman—famously fierce, deeply knowledgeable, with a faith in our ways that never ceases to inspire me, even now, years after her passing. I relied on Anna's advice and friendship; she relied on my support and help. She sensed our stress and concern as we reported on the birth of Luella.

Encouraging is not the word I'd use to describe Anna's response. She usually trampled everyone's emotions and just spoke her truth, and this time was no different. She sounded off the facts as she saw them: "I am filling my pipe right now and I am going to pray for her and the rest of you. Listen. You already know what to do. Use the Indian medicine for her first bath. Put out tobacco. Don't let those medical people do experiments on her afterbirth—that goes out in the woods. She will be okay. She will be more than okay. She will surprise you. I already had the dream for her Indian name."

We did what we were told. Luella got her first bath in a warm tea made out of namewashk (catnip). We brought her placenta home and buried it on the north side of a maple tree, the tree of life, for her health and longevity. We furnished a feast and prayer on her fourth day on earth to welcome her arrival among us. I believed in everything we were doing. But I was still concerned about Luella. My other kids had taken to nursing right away, had started putting on weight, and were active and gifted at crying at high volume. But Luella basically slept for weeks on end, nursing here and there.

Anna was unperturbed.

We had a little trouble coordinating all of my daughter's namesakes' schedules, so there was a delay, but six months after the birth, we gathered our extended family for her naming ceremony. Luella received several Ojibwe names that day, but Anna's was her first. Anna described in vivid detail the dream she had had about a woman, tall and strong, so filled with spiritual power that the eagles kept swooping, swarming, and perching on her body, all along her arms, shoulders, neck, and head. "Your daughter's name is Chi-ogimaa-binesiikwe—Big Boss Eagle Woman."

And then everything changed. Luella had basically slept for the first six months of her life, but after her naming, she didn't let anybody else sleep. She started to laugh loudly, cry loudly, nurse with gusto, and then crawl, walk, talk, scream, and boss everybody around like no kid I have ever seen. The cultural toolbox awakened something spiritually in her, and all my doubts were put to rest. Luella is fearless, confident, and strong, with a natural leadership persona that just can't be taught. Of all my kids, she is the one the world knows is utterly dauntless.

WHO ARE THE OJIBWE?

Before I take you deeper into my culture around pregnancy and childbirth, clans, Native names, and our springtime harvest practices, I need to share a little more about our tribe, since that background tapestry has fundamentally shaped our culture. In former times, an Ojibwe person would be immersed in the community and history of their people. Navigating spring (and every subsequent season) requires an understanding of the environment where spring occurs. It works that way with the seasons and with the metaphor for our journey in this book.

The DNA of Ojibwe people is truly ancient. Neither Ojibwe legends nor the archaeological community knows exactly how ancient. But we do know there is evidence of humans in North America tens of thousands of years ago. We know the glaciers retreated from the Great Lakes around eleven thousand years ago and that humans have lived in this area ever since. The remains of Minnesota Woman, an archaeological "discovery" in

Anna Gibbs holding Luella at Luella's naming ceremony. *Anton Treuer*

northwestern Minnesota, date to around ten thousand years ago. Native Americans are the indigenous people of this hemisphere—not immigrants.

But while the indigenous gene pool is truly ancient, the emergence of the Ojibwe as a collection of related cultural groups distinct from their other Indigenous cousins is much more recent. While many Native people are fond of saying that we are as old as the hills, and our distinctive languages and cultures have evolved over millennia, it was as recently as two thousand years ago that they reached a form Ojibwe people today might recognize.

Before the Ojibwe emerged as a distinct cultural and linguistic group, our ancestors probably moved around North America quite a bit in response to expanding and shrinking ice sheets. People had to go where the food was, after all. And as the human population grew, they must have run into many other people. Charles Mann and other scholars have estimated the Indigenous population of North America to have been one hundred million people when Columbus arrived (compared to an estimated European population of eighty-eight million at the time). While there isn't universal agreement about these figures, it seems likely that North America had a comparable population density to Europe. Human interactions—war and diplomacy—likely had an impact on how people moved and where they lived as well. Tom Peacock and Marlene Wisuri wrote a book called *The Good Path* in which they suggest the early ancestors of the Ojibwe came from the west to settle along the Atlantic Coast thousands of years ago. I have never personally heard a story about that from Archie Mosay or any of my other knowledgeable elders. And I have never seen archaeological evidence to confirm that, either. That does not mean that Peacock and Wisuri are wrong; I just can't validate that story within my cultural or academic understanding. What I can say with confidence is that the Ojibwe did emerge as a linguistically and culturally distinct group of people a couple thousand years ago, somewhere along the Atlantic Coast and Eastern Great Lakes.

There are many versions of the Ojibwe creation story. Some have been published in books; I reserve the full details of mine for ceremony space. But the teachings we derive from that story populate a lot of our everyday cultural practices, explain a lot about the Ojibwe worldview, and are shared more freely. The Creator is not described as male or female and goes by many names in our language. The Ojibwe word *manidoo* is usually translated as "spirit." The root *man-* pertains to creating things, including procreation—*manidiwag* means "they have sex with one another." And *-doo* pertains to "nurture." Even the word for breast, *doodoosh*, describes its function in nursing babies. So, a spirit is one who "creates and nurtures." The Creator is usually called by a name that includes *manidoo*. I often use manidoo naagaanizid, meaning "head spirit." Also common is gichi-manidoo, meaning "Great Spirit." Sounding very similar, but having a slightly different meaning, is gizhe-manidoo, meaning "kind or gentle spirit."

The Creator made things in a certain order: the sky, the sun, the stars, the moon, the many planets. And each part of the effort had its sequence as well. In making the earth, it was fire, rock, and layers of earth. In planting the earth, it was water, grass, trees. In making animate beings, it was four-legged animals, birds, creatures in the water, and last of all humans. (The Ojibwe usually consider animals to include just four-legged creatures rather than the broader English definition.) We often remind one another of the meaning this order carries. Humans were the last things placed on earth, and if we disappeared, everything else would get along just fine—in fact, probably better than before. But if anything created before us were to disappear, it would take everything created after with it. We depend on the earth, not the other way around. We are part of the web of life, not its masters.

I take this to mean that we need to be humble and considerate as we tread upon the earth. We shouldn't take things for granted. We endanger ourselves when we look at water, rocks, trees, animals, birds, and fish as resources for our use and exploitation. Humankind is not given dominion over the earth. It's the other way around.

There is a teaching that Archie frequently shared at naming ceremonies and feasts. He said that when humans were placed here on earth, we were told not to be takers. The Creator told us to respect all things (earth, water, plants) and respect all beings (legged animals, birds, swimmers, and humans), and we were given the first plant—the tobacco plant—as a tool to show that respect. Tobacco is the currency we use to pay for whatever we need to harvest. Today the Ojibwe still use either the tobacco plant or the inner bark of red willow (different plants but cultural equivalents) this way.

This is why we use tobacco for everything. If we harvest a plant, we use tobacco first. If I am picking sage, I place a pinch of tobacco by the tallest sage plant in the field. I don't pick that plant; I pick the other plants around it. If I am harvesting a maple sapling to use for a wigwam pole, I place a pinch of tobacco at the base of the sapling before I cut. If I kill a deer, I place a pinch of tobacco on the head of the deer, apologize, and explain the reason for my action (to gather food). If I want to ask someone to pray for me, I don't post on Facebook—I place a pinch of tobacco in the person's hand and explain my request. Tobacco is spiritual currency. For more complex ceremonies, it is shared with other people in a group and can be smoked in a pipe, burned in a fire, tied in cloth and hung on the wall of a house, or put in the woods. It can go in the fire, in the water, on the earth, at the base of a tree or rock. Skipping the use of tobacco is taking without paying.

All takings cause a reaction. If there is a giving (tobacco) during the taking (harvest or request), the spiritual energy is positive.

But if there is taking without the tobacco payment, the spiritual energy is negative. The result could be bad luck hunting or fishing, scarcity, or stress.

Anna Gibbs liked to a share a legend about the eagle. Since the eagle flies higher than other birds, it serves as a messenger to the Creator. Every day, the eagle reports on what Anishinaabe is doing. (The word *Anishinaabe* means a Native person, or "one of the people," but can be used collectively as well, meaning "the people.") When the eagle sees us making tobacco offerings and respecting everything in creation and one another, that report keeps us in the good graces of the manidoog (spirits). We remember the time when the people forgot to do this and the earth was cleansed with water—the great flood. But tobacco offering is not a fear-based practice; it's a positive practice with a little sense of obligation and a will to pay it forward. The eagle isn't policing us; it's watching out for us. Many people offer tobacco when they come close.

Most of my elders saw no obligation to help someone if they called on the phone. But if someone showed up at their house and offered a pinch of tobacco, they usually dropped everything to help. Many times, I saw Archie Mosay, Tom Stillday, Anna Gibbs, and others get funeral calls. Someone would be on the phone, explaining that their mom had died, that they lived 250 miles away, and then asking, "Could you drive to our community, since that's where the funeral will be anyways, and I will just give you tobacco when you get here?" Anna was usually the bluntest of them all, saying, "No. If you loved your mom, get in that car, drive up here, and give me the tobacco." They would. And she would drop everything, spend a few days in their community, accompany them to the store to get all the supplies they needed for the funeral, spend hours with the bereaved family, make sure they wrote down all of her detailed instructions in a notebook, and then sing and talk for hours at the wake and funeral with heartfelt hugs and tears of appreciation flowing from the family. Tobacco opened the door to her devoted service. If there was no tobacco, she was at the movies with her grandkids, the dollar store, or the casino.

I often get asked to speak and pray. For conferences and special events, organizers want an invocation or prayer to kick things off in a good way. But sometimes they are so busy that Ojibwe protocol slips their minds. I'm on the agenda. I show up. There is a request for a prayer. And there is no tobacco. I'm a little more understanding than some of my teachers about how easy it is to forget something like that. But it's still critical protocol. So, I usually approach that as a teaching opportunity and show them what to do. The tobacco is still required before the prayer.

The rule book is simple. Respect all things. Respect all beings. Use tobacco. What takes a little more reflection is figuring out what it means to respect all things and what it means to respect all beings. I usually use this barometer, though, when I make decisions. While there is no set of commandments in the teachings of my elders, the respect principle is a great guide. Is drinking alcohol taboo? What does it look like to respect your body and the other people around you? Common sense says either don't do it or do it in moderation. Then you're in alignment with these teachings. That's what I try to do. I don't always succeed. With regard to alcohol, I don't drink; it's not that I judge anyone who does, but I officiate at ceremonies where people come to heal from trauma and addiction. I feel my role as an officiant requires me to respect their need for a safe, sober place to heal, and if I used alcohol or drugs, I would negatively impact that experience for them. I would force them to deal with the negative consequences of my actions. So, for me, removing that obstacle is a pretty easy decision.

The respect teachings tell me to be kind and decent to other people, to tread lightly upon the earth. I can see times when we have stepped away from those teachings. At the height of the fur trade, Ojibwe people overharvested in some places or got out of balance with our teachings. But when we hold those teachings in front of us as we make decisions big and small, we are aligned with Ojibwe values and can be the best versions of ourselves.

After the creation, there is a story of the great flood. It's a cautionary tale. Life was so easy and abundant that the people forgot to use tobacco, and the Creator cleansed the earth with water and started everything anew. The second creation was modeled on the first, but there were different plants, different animals, birds, swimmers, and people. Most of what we see now is from the second creation. But there are survivors from the first still among us, like the sturgeon and the dragonfly.

The creation teachings are timeless, and to me they are not inconsistent with scientific teachings. Every generation of children is different from the one that came before. We are biologically evolving in the scientific understanding of what that means. Our craniums are getting microscopically bigger and our jaws are getting smaller with the birth of each new generation. At the same time, each birth is also a sacred and spiritual event. Our stories and teachings describe occurrences that none of us witnessed but all of us imagine. There is scientific truth in them. There was a great flood, when the ice dam went out on Hudson Bay at the end of the last ice age, ocean levels rose dramatically. Many cultures have stories to describe the experience. And in addition to the scientific truth in those stories, there is spiritual truth and guidance for us all on how to be.

The words we use in the Ojibwe language to refer to ourselves all reflect our stories of origin somehow. *Ojibwe* is the word we use to refer to our specific tribe of Natives. It was misspelled by some early French explorers and eventually written down as Chippewa. That word is still around, even in some Ojibwe tribal constitutions. It's not really offensive, just mildly erroneous and slowly working its way out as tribes, and maybe someday the US government, update their labels. Although there are dozens of attempted morphological assessments of deeper meaning behind the word Ojibwe and some are really different from one another, most have to do with the unique sound we make (our language), a geographical place-name description of where we came from, the puckered-toe moccasin of the Ojibwe people, or our unique system of writing on birchbark. We have another word, Anishinaabe, which we usually use to refer to all Indigenous people. Most of the definitions of Anishinaabe describe being created spontaneously or being the second creation of humankind.

Ojibwe is one of twenty-nine different tribes whose languages are part of the Algonquian language family and who all share common biological ancestors. All those tribes use some derivation of the word Anishinaabe for self-reference. (Even Lenni Lenape, which the Delaware use for self-reference, is the same as Anishinaabe—they use the letter *l* in many places where the Ojibwe use *n*.) Some scholars have used the term Algic to refer to the mother group, the ancestors of these twenty-nine tribes. Linguists have often used proto-Algonquian. To me, they are just the ancient ones.

While living on the Atlantic Coast and Eastern Great Lakes, the mother group came under a lot of stress. The land there was especially rich in food resources—abundant fish in the ocean and inland lakes and rivers, land well suited for Indigenous agriculture (especially corn, beans, and squash, which were staples for all of us then), many types of berries and nuts, and numerous species of small game, ducks, geese, turkeys, deer, moose, and bear. It was a diverse food production system, which also meant a stable one. If the snowshoe hare population crashed, there was still everything else to rely upon. The easy access to food led to a population boom, and that increased pressure on land and food resources. Cyclical challenges to the food supply (like a drought) sometimes created territorial conflict as people hunted harder and ranged farther to make up the difference for a crop failure. Some of the ancient ones decided to move west, where they hoped there would be less conflict over territory and resources.

There are many stories about prophets who appeared among the people at this time. Some warned about danger, about the coming of new people to their land. The late Edward Benton-Banai, author of *The Mishomis Book* and one of the medicine dance lodge chiefs in Wisconsin, described the prophecies in terms of seven fires. Each represented a historical time period. The first three fires were a time of great loss, hardship, and conflict, and they warned of a clash with people from a different land. The second three described a time when the people would lose their ways, be controlled by the newcomers, and be separated from everything they held dear. And the seventh fire described a time of rebirth, renewal, reclamation, and growth. Prophets told the people to move west to the land where food grows on water (a reference to the wild rice beds of the Western Great Lakes).

It's hard to identify the degree to which the ancient ones were motivated by the prophecies and the degree to which they were motivated by practical things such as conflict and food scarcity. But the end result was a massive migration. Over a period of hundreds of years, thousands of the ancient ones started moving west. They didn't have a specific destination—only vague descriptions of a land where food grows on water. In small groups ranging from twenty to five hundred people, they slowly migrated, establishing new villages along the way. Some stayed in the new villages for generations. Some are still there. Others pushed on. All of them encountered other Native people. Some they befriended. Some resisted their movement. Some conflicts slowed the migration, and some enabled it to proceed faster.

As the people spread out, they changed and diversified. The ancient ones became the twenty-nine Algonquian tribes and included the Odawa (Ottawa), Potawatomi, Cree, Menominee, Meskwaki (Fox), and Ojibwe. All of this happened a couple thousand years ago. By the time Europeans made it to the Eastern Great Lakes in the early 1600s, the center of the sprawling Ojibwe population was around Sault Ste. Marie. Over the next two hundred years, the Ojibwe continued to push west, forging new alliances with the Dakota, Cree, Blackfeet, and other tribes—and, at times, fighting those same tribes. Some eventually made it all the way to the Rocky Mountains.

As the French and English sparred in the Eastern Great Lakes, the British-allied Haudenosaunee (Iroquois) attacked the Ojibwe from the east. The Ojibwe eventually overpowered them, and through the course of that conflict, some moved back east, displacing their enemies and occupying some Huron lands after that tribe suffered tragic depopulation from smallpox and Haudenosaunee attacks. The Ojibwe ended up expanding their territory twentyfold over the course of the migration and conflicts, creating the massive geographical spread of the tribe and the cultural differences between various communities within it.

SEVEN GENERATIONS

Every language embodies the unique worldview of a people. Ojibwe terms of relation tell us a lot about how people think. Check out this simple list of words:

Indaanikobijigan = My great-grandparent
Nimishoomis / Nookomis = My grandfather / My grandmother
Ingitiziim = My parent
Niin = Me
Niniijaanis = My child
Noozhishenh = My grandchild
Indaanikobijigan = My great-grandchild

Looking at the terms for each of these seven generations in a family, you will see the words for great-grandparent and great-grandchild are the same. The deeper meaning of the word *indaanikobijigan* is "my line." This is more than a linguistic curiosity—it's a deeply embedded cultural belief. Everything we do crosses seven generations in a line. If there is trauma, it carries forward seven generations. If there is resilience, it carries forward seven generations. We are therefore the product of traumas and resilience seven generations back. What scientists call epigenetics, we call blood memory. In the modern world, people are encouraged to think of immediate gains—often short-term economic benefits trump long-term environmental and health consequences. But in the Ojibwe cosmos, we are to think of the impact that our actions today will have seven generations in the future. "Should we build the pipeline?" is a question best answered when we think, *How will economic and environmental trade-offs impact my line seven generations in the future?* If the potential positive economic impacts, compounding over seven generations, obviously outweigh the negative environmental repercussions over the same amount of time, then build the pipeline. But if they don't, then don't.

I think about this all the time in my cultural service and academic work. How can I ensure positive effects from my ceremonial service and language revitalization efforts ripple out seven generations into the future? Which projects will have lasting value? What cultural practices are so healing or identity creating or nourishing that I know my descendants seven generations ahead will benefit from them? Those are the ones I will spend my time on, emphasize with my kids, and share with others. It's a marvel to me that the Ojibwe still have a culture left to preserve, considering everything we have been through. But I believe that seven generations back, someone was praying for me now, wishing this toolbox upon me with all its healing and sustaining power. Today I offer tobacco and bowls of food and I pray for my relatives seven generations in the future, so that they will have the same. And I believe.

SEVEN GRANDFATHER TEACHINGS

Many Ojibwe describe a variation of the Seven Grandfather Teachings: debwewin (truth), mino-dabasenindizowin (humility), manaajitwaawin (respect), zhawendaagoziwin (love), gwayakowaadiziwin (honesty), zoongide'ewin (courage), and nibwaakaawin (wisdom). Schools, programs, and language initiatives sometimes post them in their offices or incorporate them into value statements for their organizations. Every one of these values resonates for me. But I tend to frame them a little differently than some people. I never heard Archie Mosay, Tom Stillday, Anna Gibbs, Melvin Eagle, or my other much older mentors say that these are the only values of our people or that these seven values are in a hierarchy or more important than other values. But they are important Ojibwe values nonetheless, and it's sometimes helpful to take a look at their deeper meaning.

The word *debwewin* (truth) comes from the Ojibwe roots *de*, meaning "heart" or "center," and *we*, meaning "sound." If someone tells the truth, they speak from the heart. Truth is sincerity and honesty, alignment of action with values and beliefs. It denotes real integrity. In the Western world, truth often revolves around a legal standard. If you get a rental car and purchase the extra insurance and then crash the car, you might find out that somewhere in the fine print of your contract was a stipulation that you would have to debit your own auto insurance policy before the new one kicked in. That's the opposite of the Ojibwe understanding of truth. *Debwewin* means doing what you say.

In the word *mino-dabasenindizowin* (humility), *mino* means "good," *dabas* means "low," *en* denotes a mental or emotional condition, and *dizo* is a reflexive ending meaning "of one's self." While *dabasenindizowin* can be translated as either "humility" or "low self-esteem," with the *mino*, it clearly means "positive humility."

Manaajitwaawin (respect) comes from the root *man*, "to create," and *twaa*, "belief." One who speaks the truth and walks with humility demonstrates true integrity, and that inspires the true respect of others. And it works the other way, too. When someone believes in something or someone, it shows up as respect.

Zhawendaagoziwin (love) comes from *zha*, denoting warmth, and *en*, which, as noted above, describes a mental or emotional process. Really, this word means "to empathize" or "to have compassion." A dictionary will reveal a couple of words for love in our language. In other verb forms and conjugations, I would say "Gizhawenimin" to mean "I love you," but it would literally translate as "I empathize with you" or "I have compassion for you." Dictionary entries for the root word *zhawenim* might include meanings as varied as to have compassion for, empathize with, love, bless, or pity someone. It's a tough one to translate precisely. The other word for "I love you" is *gizaagi'in*, which describes "holding close," denoting possessive love—such as between parents and children or between lovers.

Gwayakowaadiziwin (honesty) comes from *gwayak*, meaning "right" or "correct," and *aadizi*, which describes living or being. When someone's life is aligned with their beliefs, they have this kind of integrity and honesty.

Zoongide'ewin (courage) is derived from *zoong*, which means "strong," and *de*, "heart." Courage is not the absence of fear but the strength to push through fear and do what's right.

Nibwaakaawin (wisdom) comes from *ib*, pertaining to the head, and *aak*, denoting treelike strength. Mental and emotional fortitude means a disciplined mind and the ability to discern the pros and cons of life's challenges. That's true wisdom.

SYMBOLS AND METAPHORS

The Ojibwe world is full of symbols and metaphors. The circle is probably the most obvious and permeates our world. The cycle of seasons and cardinal points of the compass revolve in a circle. So do the earth, the moon, and the sun. We sit in circles for ceremonial, social, and political occasions. We start our life cycle as dependents, and often by the time we are elders we become dependent again—full circle. We usually start life with no teeth, and a lot of us end up losing them in the end as well. Traffic at ceremonies usually is directed clockwise around the circle, just like a natural progression around the cardinal directions, from east to south to west to north.

The circle is a common metaphor for other Native American groups and many others around the world. People share their cultures. Within Native circles, a tribe that has suffered from assimilation is more likely to borrow teachings, ceremonies, and metaphors from a neighboring tribe because those teachings resonate and there aren't enough cultural resources in the home community to keep the culture of origin intact. When that happens, the more widely available and most easily accessible pan-Indian teachings gain the most traction.

Many Lakota teachings have spread not just throughout the Plains but all over Indian country. There are even white people in Germany trying to do Lakota stuff. Lakota teachings about the medicine wheel, which uses the circle metaphor and integrates teachings about the four seasons, four compass points, and four stages of life, resonate well with Ojibwe cultural teachings. The only problem I have with the medicine wheel is that while it seems to sync with my Ojibwe teachings in many ways, I never once heard my deeply knowledgeable elders use that specific metaphor in Ojibwe ceremonies or space (and I asked a lot of questions of a lot of really knowledgeable folk). In some parts of Ojibwe country, especially Sault Ste. Marie and places east of there, where the missionaries were working the longest, the medicine wheel has been accepted into the Ojibwe culture kit. But in my area and for me, it really hasn't. There's nothing wrong with it, but my cultural toolbox is complete without it and there is no void that needs to be filled with Lakota teachings, beautiful though they may be.

The Ojibwe also use the symbol of an open hand, palm facing out, with all fingers extended, in a number of contexts. Before European contact, the Ojibwe did not commonly shake hands when they greeted one another; they just opened their hands and held them up to one another. Today, I shake hands with Native and non-Native people all the time, but I do simply open my hand to greet fellow Natives at times, too. It is partially practical (if I'm moving fast or at a distance) and partially cultural—an Indigenous affirmation. During the COVID-19 pandemic, there was an obvious health benefit. On the ceremonial drums an outstretched hand represents people greeting the Creator and the Creator greeting the people. It has other ceremonial applications as well.

Recent activism to raise awareness about missing and murdered Indigenous women uses a hand symbol, too, usually the image of a red hand painted over the mouth. That has a different origin and use, though. In that usage, the hand symbolizes the silencing of women, and the imagery is designed to evoke awareness.

We have a saying in Ojibwe: "Giishpin wiikaa ani-zagaakwaag gibimaadiziwin, aabajitoon giwaagaakwad." It means: "If there is ever a bramble in your life, use your ax." The ax (or sometimes the hatchet) is seen as a metaphor for our ways—when things get hard, we pick up our ways. If there is stress, struggle, depression, grief, or trauma, we are to go to drum ceremonies, or put tobacco down in the woods by a rock or tree or in the water. It's been a great guidepost for me. I sometimes want to retreat from the world when I feel wounded, but thinking of the ax helps get me out of seething with anger, moping and feeling sorry for myself, or shutting down. I think in the non-Native world, people often feel pressure to check their problems at the door and pretend that everything is fine. They put on a veneer of functionality that makes it harder to process tough emotions. In the Ojibwe world, we are told to bring our problems into the circle, and everyone else will help share the load. It's at the heart of what it means to be communal—the ax is good medicine.

There are sacred numbers in Ojibwe as well. There are *twelve* feathers on eagle's tail. There are *seven* generations, seven original clans, and seven grandfather teachings. There are *four* seasons, four points on the compass, four winds, four layers of sky, four layers of earth, four phases of life. It takes *two* people to make a baby, drum chiefs are usually seated in pairs, and there is duality in the sun and moon, sky and earth, fire and water. And there is *one* Creator.

CODED MEANINGS

Words in the Ojibwe language, like words in other languages, are composed of smaller roots or morphemes that often carry coded meanings, deeper cultural concepts, or even literary references. I share many examples throughout the book to give you a better understanding of what words really mean. They speak powerfully to our cultural concepts.

Sometimes a word has a whole story behind it. For example, we have a story about a bird who had feathers of every color in the rainbow—bright, conspicuous, glorious feathers. He also had the most beautiful singing voice of all the birds. It was enchanting. All the creatures on earth admired this bird, and Anishinaabe most of all. The bird loved them all back and loved Anishinaabe most of all. One winter it was terribly cold. The people were suffering from the cold. What food they could find was so frozen that they couldn't eat it. They had no fire—no way to cook food or heat their lodges. The bird pitied the people and resolved to help them. He flew up into the sky, higher and higher. He wanted to approach the sun and retrieve its warmth for the people. He flew for a long time until he was close enough to feel the heat of the sun. Soon it grew so hot that it started to singe his beautiful feathers. But he didn't turn back, and he didn't quit. He flew and flew until he reached the sun. His feathers were burned black, and his throat was seared by the heat. But he made it. He retrieved fire and brought it back to earth and gave it to the people.

Now the people had something to cook their food and warm their lodges. They were so grateful. The bird never recovered his former glory from his sacrificial ordeal, but he lived. We call this bird aandeg, which means "he who changes in the light." In English he is known as the crow. His feathers are as black as charcoal. His voice is rough and raspy. But when the sun shines on him, there is glint of multiple colors in his dark feathers, a hint of his former glory.

The crow is a common bird; eagles and bears get much more admiration. But when we speak Ojibwe, the word *aandeg* invokes this whole story. It's oral literary reference built right into the language. And the language is full of stories like this.

SPIRITS

When we bring children into the world, they usually grow up to become fully capable people. In time, they can advise us and even take care of us. This offers a parallel to the Ojibwe cosmos. There is one Creator for all things, who made a number of spirits. Just as it works for human parents with several children, the Creator then called upon these spirits and gave them jobs. The Creator placed some among us here on earth to watch over the water, the trees, the rocks. One was placed in each of the four cardinal directions, in the form of a distinct and powerful wind. Other spirits were placed in a council with the Creator, and these the Creator began to consult in all important decisions.

For most of our everyday ceremonies, we invoke not only the Creator but also these spirits here on earth, near and among us. Some take care of our health or of the wild rice. They serve as intermediaries and helpers. Ojibwe prayers are notoriously long-winded in part because we take the time to mention around thirty spirits and their functions in watching over, healing, and helping us. This adds to, rather than diminishes, our faith in a common Creator.

SMARTPHONES AND CEREMONIES

Almost everyone now has a smartphone. They are so powerful and do so many things: entertain, inform, addict, and disrupt. I run my professional life with mine, and a fair amount of my social life, too. But when it is ceremony time, phones have some special considerations in Ojibwe space.

Joseph Nayquonabe Sr. explained to me that the spirits are very powerful but easily confused and distracted. When we set dates for ceremonies, we often offer tobacco and food and pray just to communicate to the spirits when we will be doing something so they show up and tune in when we need their help. Spirits are, like people, sometimes shy. They are, like people, often attracted to music and sounds: the drum, the rattle, and the human voice. We ask people to shut off their smartphones when it's ceremony time not just so the lights and sounds don't distract us—we also don't want the lights and sounds to distract the spirits. Maybe they'll go check out the phone's ringer or song instead of the ceremonial song.

We also come to ceremony to ground in our Native space, not to be distracted by the rest of the world. We go there to heal from injuries and traumas that happen in the rest of the world. So, we often have people check their phones at the door before we even start.

THE GREAT SPIRIT'S PLAN

Every culture has its own way of answering the question "Are our lives guided by random luck, good and bad choices, or the Creator's plan for us?" From everything I have learned about our Ojibwe ways and all my life experiences, I have to say that it is all of the above. There is an element of luck that affects our lives. Some people are born in parts of the world that are riddled with war or famine. It wasn't their bad choice or poor morals that put them there, and it couldn't be the Creator's plan unless the Creator is either powerless, uncaring, or cruel. But that's not the only thing going on. When someone gets drunk, drives ninety miles an hour, and dies in a fiery car crash, that wasn't bad luck. It was a bad choice (or series of bad choices). The Creator didn't will that outcome. The person put themselves in that position, and there was a terrible consequence. But that, too, is not the only thing that's going on.

The Creator does have a plan for us all. We may be like ants on an anthill who struggle to get the Creator's attention at times. Good luck, bad luck, random luck, good choices, bad choices, and everything between can deeply impact our trajectory in life and our longevity. But in addition to our innate gifts, we all have some measure of destiny. It's so hard to see what that is, and there are so many things in the way of our spiritual sight—but when we find it and embrace it, the results can be truly astonishing. In the Ojibwe world we get glimpses of this in our dreams or visions when we are fasting. We pay close attention to those things because they can tell us much about ourselves and what direction we should go. Archie paid close attention to his dream when I walked through the door. And I have paid close attention to mine.

As I go about my life, I try to listen, to intuit, to look for signs and be willing to be spiritually guided. At the same time, I try to make good choices about what I eat, how I exercise, and what kinds of risks I am willing to take. I have goals and try to do things with intention. But I never assume that I know better than the Creator what is best for me.

Even when I pray, I usually frame my prayer as a request to be guided as to my best course of action rather than a request for a specific result. I went through a divorce and custody proceeding a couple decades ago. Rather than asking for custody of my daughter, I just asked the Creator to show me what to do and to provide my daughter with her best chance at a long, healthy, happy life. She ended up spending half her time with me and half with her mother, growing up feeling deeply loved by both of us. The sayings "Be careful what you ask for—you just might get it" and "Thank God for unanswered prayers" resonate with me.

I try to be mindful of my thoughts, especially when I am praying or at ceremony. There are powerful spirits around at those times, and I don't want a stray thought to manifest as a desire, a desire as a prayer, a prayer that creates a consequence. When my pipe bowl is connected to the stem of my pipe, it's like a bullhorn for my thoughts and prayers, so I have a divider in my pipe bag to keep them separated when I'm not ready for prayer time. A lot of other Ojibwe people do this, too, often by wrapping the bowl in cloth before placing it in the pipe bag.

Because tobacco is considered spiritual currency for prayer requests and harvest offerings, I have always felt a little weird about social smoking. I don't judge anyone. Both of my parents were smokers, and they both paid health consequences for that habit. But my concern goes deeper. What happens if you smoke tobacco without carefully minding your thoughts? Could the tobacco add extra spiritual weight to what you're thinking when you smoke? What if you are smoking and drinking? Or trying to pick someone up at a bar? I am not saying that a situation like this would negate someone's free will, choices, or any of the other things that impact a person's life. But I like to be careful with my thoughts and prayers, especially when tobacco is involved.

As I think about the power of luck, choices, and the Great Spirit's plan, I believe our everyday actions create habits. Those habits persist and create our character. So, one of the keys to a spiritual life is creating spiritual actions and spiritual habits.

FEAST FOOD

Ceremony food is often thought of much like tobacco. It's an offering. Tobacco is the base payment for a prayer or the harvest of a plant, animal, bird, or fish; food is an additional offering that adds extra weight to the payment. Because of this, Ojibwe feast food has a few rules. For starters, it doesn't go in the garbage. If people cannot clean their plates, leftover food can be stored and reheated and eaten later, but whatever doesn't get consumed has to be taken care of in a clean way. It can go in a fire to be burned. It can be placed in the water. Or it can be placed next to a tree in a clean place. Wherever the food that is being "put out" goes, it should be somewhere dogs won't eat it.

At Red Lake and some other places, apples are not included in feast food because they are associated with the Christian story of Adam and Eve and the forbidden fruit. Some worry that their inclusion might signal a mixing of religious traditions, which is usually taboo. In most parts of Wisconsin and Mille Lacs, that is not a concern, and you'll find apple pies and other apple dishes at a lot of feasts.

We have a legend about Wenabozho (referred to as Nenabozho in northern Ojibwe communities), a being who was half human and half spirit and walked the earth with a wolf, naming everything in creation. When their work was done, they parted ways, but whatever happened to one would happen to the other. Both were misunderstood, hunted almost to extinction, but resilient, supportive of others in the pack, and making a comeback. Our parallel lives were not to cross again, so we keep dogs (cousins of the wolf) away from ceremonies and away from ceremony food.

PREGNANCY AND CHILDBIRTH

Now that you've had a chance to explore the cultural environment of the Ojibwe, we can shift focus to the cultural beliefs and practices of spring—the season of new life. In our creation story, the human body is made out of earth. It's a cup, temporary housing for our souls. The body is animated by the arrival of a spirit—the unique energy, light, breath, and sound of each human. This makes pregnancy a special and sacred time.

Pregnancy marks a powerful transition. While the body of the new baby is growing in utero, the spirit of the new baby is not yet lodged inside the body. It is hovering around the pregnant mother, almost like it is still attached to the spirit world by an umbilical cord. When baby is born and takes their first breath, the cord connecting the spirit to the spirit world severs, and it inhabits the child's body for the rest of their life.

Expectant mothers have a wide range of taboos and guidance. The spirit of the baby is already present throughout pregnancy. If the baby is a girl, the eggs for the babies that girl may have are already inside of her while she is inside her mother—three generations in one woman. Mothers and fathers are encouraged to sing to their babies in utero, which has both practical and spiritual effects—after birth, babies recognize the sounds of their parents' voices immediately.

There are food taboos, too. There is a saying that if an expectant mother eats too many strawberries, it can give the baby red birthmarks. There is also a taboo against telling winter legends out of season, for all people at all times. It is said that if someone violates the taboo, a giant toad may mark the storyteller with blue welts, and those marks can be passed through generations. Some say that certain birthmarks—slate-gray nevi, blue spots on a baby's body that look like bruises—are the result. Those blue birthmarks are very common in Native babies, and they disappear after a few years. All my kids had them. Maybe someone was telling legends out of season in my line, back in the day.

Just a few generations back, Ojibwe women worked hard throughout pregnancy simply because they had to. Today, that is still the case for some Ojibwe women, but even those for whom it is not are encouraged to be busy and physically active throughout pregnancy. The doctors are catching up to our elders on that teaching now, too.

Most Ojibwe ceremonies around death are off-limits or restricted for expectant mothers. They usually avoid going to wakes and funerals unless it is unavoidable, such as because of the death of a very close relative. Even if it's a close relative, expectant mothers usually do not approach the casket or view the body of the deceased. Likewise, babies and young children are usually discouraged from attending funerals. It is said that everybody loves a brand-new baby, even the souls of the departing. Out of fear that the departing soul might want to take a sweet baby with them, people usually don't take a chance and stay away from death-related ceremonies.

In former times, Ojibwe people had a lot of fear about infant mortality. Baby showers were never thrown before a child was born. While prospective parents hoped and prayed for a healthy baby, they never expected it, and a shower before the birth would be like taking a positive outcome for granted. That teaching is hard for some expectant mothers. But having a nursery all prepared and no baby to bring home makes a miscarriage or stillbirth even harder.

Because there is a widespread belief that the spirit of an unborn child is hovering around the mother throughout pregnancy rather than directly inhabiting the body of the fetus, miscarriages and stillbirths in Ojibwe culture are typically not handled with full-fledged funeral rites. These are still terrible losses, especially late in a pregnancy, and the customs for handling loss and grief (shared later in this book) still apply. My wife, Blair, miscarried at twelve weeks, and we had a lot of conversations with my mentors about the proper protocols for this. In the end, we wrapped the tiny body of the baby in red cloth and had a small ceremony in the woods before placing it in a tree. We were told that since baby wasn't really fully here just yet, this symbolized the connection the spirit had with the spirit world and was different from the funeral custom of burial to symbolize the return of the body (which is made of earth) back to the earth. If a baby has taken even one breath, however, the spirit has entered the child's body, and standard funeral rites are customary.

There are many varied teachings about childbirth in the Ojibwe world, and a lot of Native doulas and midwives actively work with Native mothers so they can have Indigenous-focused birth plans. Families may bring a little moss to the birth and place the baby on it immediately after arrival to bond the child with mother earth. I was instructed to make sure all of my children had their first bath administered by the family, rather than a nurse. We used a medicine, namewashk (catnip), that is abundant in our area. It has a faint minty, almost licorice-like smell. We boiled the medicine and strained out the leaves to make a tea that we used for the bath. The medicine serves mainly to strengthen the physical constitution of the baby. But after exhilarating and exhausting birth experiences for every one of my children, the bath also let us turn our full attention to every detail of the baby. (One of ours was even born with hair on her butt!) When I washed my babies and combed the vernix out of their hair, they stared at me, and I fell instantly in love. Babies need that. Parents need that. The result is not just a physically healthier baby but parents who are even more highly motivated to do whatever that baby needs.

After each of our children's births, we took the placenta home and then went out in the woods to bury it on the north side of a maple tree with tobacco. Some Ojibwe people bury the placenta on the east side, and some prefer a white pine (a symbol of longevity) over the maple. I was taught that the maple is the tree of life. Life cycles start in the east but come full circle in the north. Our family has harvested maple sap to make into syrup and sugar in the same place for my entire life. It's an amazing feeling when we go to the sugarbush every spring. My children are pulling life (in the form of maple sap) from the trees where their placentas are buried.

Once the healthy baby has arrived, some families go home and make war whoops or even fire guns in the air. It's finally time to celebrate. In addition to the normal stream of visitors and well-wishers, the parents have a number of ceremonies to plan.

We use medicines for most of the troubleshooting that arises. We use wanak (sumac berries) to make a tea to help treat a hemorrhage. We use the roots of raspberry plants to boil a tea to help with milk flow.

Mothers are encouraged to breastfeed, which in the Ojibwe world is considered the child's first formal teaching. Nourishment comes first from the mother. Since the word for breast, *doodoosh*, is derived from the root *doo*, pertaining to nurture, the word for milk, *doodooshaaboo* (breast fluid), literally means "nurture fluid."

The parents sponsor a feast four days after the birth to announce the birth and thank the Creator and helping spirits among us for the arrival of a new spirit in the world. Since we don't hold a baby shower before birth, this ceremony often provides the first chance for people to give gifts to the baby. The fear of infant mortality generated a number of customs, and we always honor them. Often someone presented our babies with new moccasins at the four-day feast. We always put a little hole in the bottom of the moccasins; this ancient custom is designed to tell the spirits, "Our baby is so poor that they already have holes in their moccasins." It invokes a protection, or pass-over, for anything that might take the baby away. The Ojibwe tradition is also not to make a cradleboard for the first baby born in a family for four weeks. Like not having a baby shower, it's a way of saying that nobody is counting blessings before they are secure. After the first month, the cradleboard is made and can be used for all subsequent children without restriction.

We kept the stubs of the umbilical cords for all of our babies, placing them in tiny pouches and hanging them off the crash bar on their cradleboard or on their swing. The Ojibwe custom is to keep those for one year. After that, they can be kept as a memento. Failure to do this might leave the child growing up looking for their belly button. They might look through the cupboards or medicine cabinets when going to strangers' houses as an adult and not even know why.

We always wrapped our babies up tight. Hospital nurses do this, too, because it comforts newborns—they are pretty confined when in the womb, so being swaddled feels normal. But the Ojibwe custom is to keep up with the swaddling much longer than in mainstream America. It teaches the child self-control as well as comfort. Some families use a waaboozoo-waaboowayaan, a rabbit-skin blanket, under the swaddle, at least in the winter. The rabbit skins for the waaboozoo-waaboowayaan are cut in long circular strips and pulled straight; when they dry, each long circular strip curls into a tube about three to four feet long. Those fur tubes are woven together. The end result is a blanket with rabbit fur on both sides that is highly prized, incredibly soft, and very warm.

Sometimes there are unusual birth situations. If a child is born with teeth or a patch of gray hair, it is believed they were touched by the ancient ones. It can be a sign that the child will grow up with some sort of special spiritual gift or higher-level wisdom.

In Ojibwe we call a twin *niizhoode*, which means "two-hearted." While each twin has their own soul and their own body, by sharing a womb and birth experience the two are spiritually connected—two hearts in one spiritual experience. Usually when twins age, they will go through major ceremonies together: having naming ceremonies at the same time, fasting at the same time, being initiated into sacred societies at the same time, and so forth.

CLANS

Clans are central to Ojibwe identity and culture. They are animals, birds, or fish. The clan doubles as the symbol for a family's ancestral line and a spiritual guide, and in former times, it was a primary determining factor in what positions someone would be groomed for—chieftainship, medicinal knowledge, or military protection. There are many words in our language with the morpheme, or root, *de*: *ode'* (heart), *ode'imin* (strawberry), *oodena* (village), *dewe'igan* (drum), and *doodem* (clan). *De* means "heart" or "center." The heart is the center of the human body; a strawberry is a heart-shaped fruit; the village is the center of the people; the drum is the heartbeat of the people. *Doodem*, formed by this morpheme meaning "heart" together with *doo*, meaning "to nurture," is the heart of someone's spiritual identity.

I defer to Archie Mosay's teachings on most cultural questions, and Archie said the very first family of humans comprised seven men and seven women, all brothers and sisters to one another. The Great Spirit set them into seven pairs to form seven new families. Each was given a guardian to watch over them—the first seven clans. And from then on, it was taboo to marry one's biological or clan relatives.

The prohibition against marrying someone of the same clan is still a major one for Ojibwe people today. Even if someone meets a clan relative from a thousand miles away and has no known biological connection to them, it is taboo to date or marry that person.

Archie said the original clans were crane, loon, fish, bear, marten, deer, and bird. These are the same as the original clans that Edward Benton-Banai recorded in *The Mishomis Book*. William Warren, who collected oral histories from Ojibwe elders in Minnesota in the 1840s, said there were five original clans rather than seven. Today there are over twenty. Some clans emerged among the Ojibwe because of intermarriage with people from other tribes. The kingfisher clan was introduced at Red Lake when a teenage Dakota boy old enough to know his Dakota clan was adopted into the tribe; the wolf clan was introduced in St. Croix River Valley communities in similar fashion, through the marriage of a Dakota man and an Ojibwe woman. Other clans are considered offshoots from one of the original ones. For example, the deer, moose, and caribou clans are thought to have all descended from the original deer clan.

There are stories about people who violated the taboo against marrying someone of the same clan. Archie told me that many people from the deer clan did this long ago. The men from one of the warrior clans, the marten, rose up and killed all the males from the deer clan in that area and then adopted everyone else into their families. Some other versions of the story claim it was the moose clan that broke the taboo and suffered the consequences. Today a violation of the clan taboo cannot be enforced by killing violators, but those who do violate it (I have met a couple of couples who did) are usually objects of reproach, similar to people who marry a sibling or first cousin. The children of people who violate the clan taboo are said to often struggle with fertility issues.

Ojibwe clans are strictly patrilineal—they are passed down through the father. Other tribes have different customs, but this is universal for the Ojibwe. Today it is not uncommon for someone who was adopted out of the community or lived outside of our normal cultural practices not to know their father's clan. In a case like that, the person is encouraged to go to a shake tent ceremony to find out what their clan is. At this ceremony, the practitioner will go inside a small tent, which is about four feet in diameter but up to twelve feet high. They speak directly to spirits and, through them, access someone's genealogy and tell them their clan. Because of the patrilineal tradition, if someone does not know their clan, they cannot just take the clan of their mother; the same is true if someone has a non-Native father.

I learned from Archie that an Ojibwe person with a non-Native father is automatically adopted into the eagle clan. I've heard different descriptions of the reason why the eagle is the adopting clan for people with non-Native fathers. One is that the eagle is kind and loving and always watching over Anishinaabe. Another is that the eagle is part of the Great Seal of the United States and seen as an emblem of the non-Native family. There are different teachings in other parts of Ojibwe country. In parts of Canada, the adopting clan is the marten, a tradition that likely stems from the story of the marten clan wiping out the male deer clan members and adopting their children into the marten clan. Some of the Michigan Ojibwe have used a chicken as the adopting clan, since the chicken came from across the ocean, like all non-Native people.

When there is a ritual adoption, the person who is adopting someone into their family has the right to confer their clan upon them. This is done through the adoption ceremony. The only exception to this is that non-Native people cannot carry Ojibwe clans—conferring clan by adoption is a gift that only carries to other Natives.

In former times, someone's clan influenced what they would do with their lives. Originally, the loon and crane clans dominated the civil chieftainships across Ojibwe country. The loon was considered the lesser chief. The loon has the pretty voice and represents diplomacy—seeking to understand and be understood. The crane was the primary chief and represented command. Often at a treaty signing or other political events, the loons did most of the talking, and talked first. The crane spoke last, often communicating that now that the loons have helped everyone understand our position, here is what we are going to do. As the Ojibwe moved from east to west in the great migration of the Algonquian peoples, sometimes new villages were settled by people who were not from one of the original chief clans. In such cases, the people had to pick chiefs from who was there, and once those new chieftainships were established, succession was usually hereditary. As a result, Mille Lacs and St. Croix have had chiefs from the bullhead and wolf clans. Leech Lake and Red Lake have had chiefs from the bear clan. Spiritual leaders often emerged from various bird clans. Warriors were often marten or bear clan.

Over time, the Ojibwe territorial expansion changed the way clans worked in our historic communities. Today, a person's clan is much less prescriptive for what kinds of positions they might be called to. There are political and spiritual leaders of many different clans. There are warriors of many clans, too.

I am from the eagle clan. And I do live a life of spiritual service to others by officiating at various ceremonies. But I'm a college professor and many other things, too. I feel like I channel my clan in a lot of the work I do, but I don't feel controlled by it. Likewise, I often think of our leadership clans, the loon and crane. While I am eagle clan, I try to channel Ojibwe teachings exhibited by leadership clans in how I lead. I usually open communication with others with the loon—I try to be kind, understanding, and diplomatic. But I'm willing to bring out some crane when I need to and be strong in my beliefs and boundaries.

NAMING

Receiving an Ojibwe name is a deeply important ceremony. Customs vary across Ojibwe country, but the significance of having a Native name, sometimes called a spirit name, is universal. It is a spiritual identifier; getting a name is like getting introduced to spiritual guardians who will be there for life. Furthermore, it establishes a relationship between the name giver and the name receiver that can be one of the most important relationships in a person's life.

I have described how we can think of a person's body as a cup—a vessel that holds their soul. The word for body, *niiyaw*, describes this function. The word for namesake, *niiyawe'enh*, is built from the same root. If someone gives someone else a name, they are in essence taking something sacred from their vessel and putting it into the other person's. Both bodies, name giver and receiver, house the same spiritual gift.

For the first few months of a baby's life, the child's cry sounds like the shortened version of the word for namesake—*we'enh, we'enh, we'enh*. It is often said that newborns are crying for namesakes. As babies get a little older, the volume and variety of their cries change. New parents are encouraged to get namesakes picked for the baby as soon as possible after the birth.

Archie said that children need one name and one namesake to give it, but they can have as many as seven names and seven namesakes. The only spiritual requirement for someone to be a namesake is that they have an Ojibwe name themselves; otherwise, the coaching part of the namesake relationship would be like learning how to drive from someone who has never done it. And the spiritual giving part of the relationship would be like opening a present and discovering that it's an empty box—a gesture without substance.

Both parents are encouraged to pick namesakes, and namesakes can be any gender or age. Since namesakes serve as spiritual guides and mentors, Blair and I usually picked more female namesakes for our girls to coach and teach them about what it means to be a woman. And for the same reasons we picked more male namesakes for our boys. But all of our kids had both male and female namesakes. We all need to learn from both men and women. We also tended to pick knowledgeable people, many of them older, for this role. But we made sure to pick at least one or two namesakes who weren't too old, so our children would be more likely to have namesakes still living as they aged into adulthood and elder namesakes passed away.

The parents pass tobacco to all namesakes, even if it means a lot of running around. The tobacco opens a spiritual connection with the name giver. Some people who give Ojibwe names wait until they receive tobacco and then pray and pay attention to their dreams, often picking a name that comes directly from a dream.

At the naming ceremony, the parents sponsor a feast. They pass tobacco to all namesakes and make a plate of food for each. There is a prayer. Each namesake also makes a pledge to be there for the name receiver for life—to pray for them, to support them, to share teachings and love. When a child is young, namesakes are usually good for a dollar at the powwow to buy a treat. When the child transitions into adulthood, they are there for coming-of-age ceremonies. They often teach everyday skills as well—hunting, trapping, ricing, sewing, moccasin making, and so forth.

Each namesake then gives the child a name. Names are quite varied. Some come from dreams; some come from a vision someone had when they were fasting; some name givers will give their own Ojibwe name to the child and both will share the same name. The parents never pick the names or even try to influence which names will be chosen in any way. Really, the names come from the spirits, and the name givers communicate on behalf of those spirits to explain the meaning behind the names. If a name giver has a dream about a bear, the name might be Bear. Often, animals, birds, and fish make strong Ojibwe names. People often give names associated with weather events, too—Thunder, Thunderbird, Wind, Rain. Others have to do with the earth—Strong Ground, Center of the Earth Woman. Many describe the movement of a bird or spirit—Flash of the Feathers, Soaring Thunderbird. Some describe human movement, especially a spirit in a sitting or standing position—He Who Sits in Front, Stands Strong. Many names are gender neutral, although a lot of women's names have the female marker *-kwe* at the end of them and get translated that way—Star Woman, Woman Standing in Four Directions. Some names are directly associated with certain colors, and the person who receives the name is instructed to incorporate those colors into their powwow regalia and ribbon shirts or ceremony skirts later in life. Some names also come with special instructions. For example, if someone has a name that is associated with thunderbirds, they may be told to put out tobacco every time it starts thundering.

There is a story behind each name—a dream or a vision of some kind. But there is no way to pack everything from a dream into one name. So, the name reflects a significant part of the dream, enough to spiritually identify the person being named without overexposing their intimate spirituality. If someone has a dream about a ceremony where people are sitting around a fire, smoking a pipe, and praying, and the smoke goes up through an opening in the clouds, the name might be Hole in the Day. In former times, Ojibwe people were sometimes careful about sharing the stories behind their names with strangers. It would be like giving someone your Social Security number on the first date. The nature of the names was to give enough information, but not too much. Marlene Stately and other elders I worked with were sometimes reluctant to share all of their names or the stories behind them. Marlene had one she agreed to share with the rest of the world—Anangookwe (Star Woman). She kept the rest to herself. For me and many other Ojibwe people today, the use of our Native names is part of our effort to affirm and empower one another as Ojibwe people. It's a decolonizing and affirming effort to call one another by our Ojibwe names.

Each namesake also gives teachings to the new baby about Ojibwe values and culture on the naming day. While the baby is usually too young to understand the words, we believe that these teachings also flow into their vessel (body) with goodness. The teachings are then inside their body and can be called up later in life. The namesakes have pledged to provide reinforcement of these teachings throughout life, helping the name receiver's mind process, learn from, and expand upon everything they receive during the ceremony.

Among the teachings we give are those discussed elsewhere in the spring section: reminders to respect all things and respect all beings, to use tobacco. We explain that there are transitions throughout our lives, and we encourage the baby to reach out to their namesakes when these times come—fasting, first kill feasts, getting the first menstrual period. We explain about the balance and rotation between seasons—spring, summer, fall, and winter. We ask the Creator and all the helping spirits to bless the baby to see all their seasons, to have a long, healthy, happy life.

Namesakes may give small gifts to the child. Anna Gibbs often gave eagle and bird names and liked to give each of her namesakes an eagle feather to hang on the wall near the baby's crib for protection. The parents usually give a gift to each namesake, too—blankets most commonly.

While getting Ojibwe names as a baby is the custom, not everyone gets to have this cultural experience as a child. It's never too late. Some people get names at a shake tent, at a sweat lodge, while fasting, or at a namesake ceremony they've requested later in life. When someone has a lot of namesakes who have passed away, they might ask for another one as an adult. Getting additional names does not erase other names—it's an additive process.

My daughter Madeline had four namesakes at her first naming ceremony. Archie passed away just months after she got her name. A few years later, at a drum ceremony in Mille Lacs, she was being chatty and loud and I was trying to shush her so her friendly chatter wouldn't interfere with the ceremony. Sitting right in front of us was Melvin Eagle, one of the drum chiefs there. She started pointing at him, saying, "Dad, look. That's my we'enh." He wasn't her namesake and I didn't want a scene, so I smiled and kept telling her to be quiet. But she was insistent, "That's my we'enh. Hi, we'enh!" Melvin turned around and told me, "She wants me to be her namesake." And that was that. I passed him tobacco, and a few weeks later he gave her another Ojibwe name.

We use our spirit names for everything. It's how we pray for people. Native names are used at all ceremonies. Funerals are conducted in the Ojibwe language and always use one of the deceased's Native names as the identifier. If someone passes away without having been through a naming ceremony, a name cannot be given after their passing. Instead, it is common practice to use a loan name (the same one) for all who passed without being named just to get them through the funeral and off to the spirit world.

When I was a child, I was first named Makoons (Little Bear) by Clement Beaulieu, a World War I veteran from my ancestral village of Bena who was quite old. He passed away a couple years after my naming. As a teenager, I passed tobacco to Mary Roberts, from Roseau River First Nation in Manitoba, to give me another. She

At Madeline's naming ceremony. Back row: Sheila LaFriniere, Anton Treuer, Robert Treuer, Margaret Treuer; front row: Dennis Jones, Archie Mosay, Veronica Hvezda, Dora Ammann. *Dan Mosay*

named me Waagosh (Fox). She became an important mentor and guide to me for many years after that.

CHILDHOOD

We have a teaching about feathers that serves as a great metaphor for life. The topside of a feather is convex—each side slopes down and away from the quill. If you imagine the quill of the feather as a path, it's easy to see how someone who strays off that path can easily be swept far away from it. That's what life is like for a lot of people who live without a community or a way of being. If you flip the feather over, however, the quill shaft is even more visible and the rest of the feather is concave, sloping up from the quill. If this is the path, when someone strays from the course, they will naturally drift back to the center. This is what it's like when you do have community and a way of being.

At naming ceremonies children are often given their first feather. It functions to protect the child and usually gets hung on the wall where they sleep or is stored nearby. In addition to protecting the baby, it works like a slow trickle charge of energy, instilling the feather teaching in the child.

A lot of Ojibwe families use a cradleboard or Indian swing for their newborns. Cradleboards are enjoying resurging use as young families look for the best ways to decolonize the child-raising experience. The back of the cradleboard is solid wood. Many people use cedar for this, since it is light, straight grained, and easy to work. Cedar is also medicinal in the Ojibwe world, but there is no spiritual requirement for its use. A footrest keeps a swaddled baby from slipping down and off the cradleboard at the bottom. A crash bar at the top ensures the baby won't get injured if the cradleboard slips. It can double as a shade canopy when it's sunny. Baby gets swaddled and then wrapped into the cradleboard. Cradleboards are usually carried around on a person's back; a tumpline fitted over the carrier's forehead places the weight on the spine. But it's quite versatile. Parents even tie the tumpline right onto a tree when visiting or working with their hands. The tight swaddling in cradleboards provides practical benefits. The child feels secure and fusses less. It's easy to move around with the kid. The structure helps cultivate good posture, too. The child gets swaddled up for the cradleboard, but they don't spend all their time in one—they have to poop and get changed, exercise, play, and crawl.

A friend and mentor of mine named Nancy Jones had twin sons, Daniel and Dennis, who ended up being some of my great friends over the past few decades. Nancy had heard that it was customary to place a small block of wood between the heels of a baby when swaddling the child in cradleboard. Being just a little skeptical, she decided to experiment and used the block with one twin but not the other. Dan (who got the block) grew up with feet that were slightly pigeon-toed, a little broader in the shoulders, and with a straight back. You really did want Dan in your canoe when it was time to portage. Dennis grew up slightly bowlegged, and he is just a little smaller in frame.

Blair and I used a cradleboard for our kids, but we had a swing for them, too, and the swing probably got even more use. The design is simple—two ropes, one blanket, and two sticks. The sticks keep it from collapsing on the baby and stop the blanket from slipping. We usually set up the swing in a corner and attached a rope. We swaddled the babies up tight and let them nap in the swing, giving the rope a tug when they stirred. That's how I made it through graduate school and watched football games for years. The swing bought a lot of peace.

When our babies got constipated, we gave them catnip tea. We used sumac berry tea when they had diarrhea. In former times, Ojibwe mothers gently pinched the lips of their children when they cried to teach them how to control tantrums and crying.

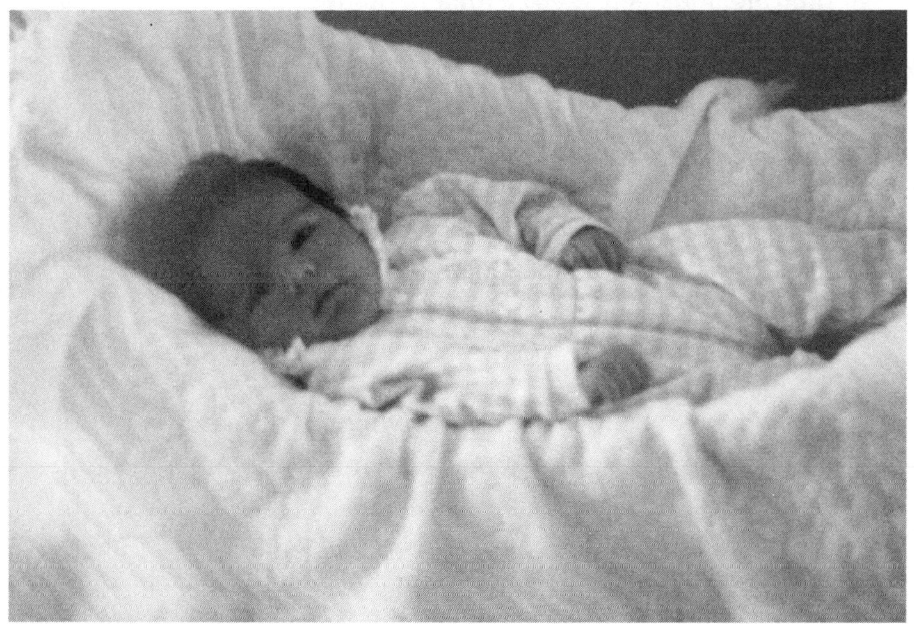

Madeline in our rope swing. ***Anton Treuer***

When game was scarce or enemies were close, that kind of control was life and death. We never did this with our kids. If I needed to go hunting, I just left them with a babysitter, until they were old enough to come along.

When a child loses a tooth, the Ojibwe used to take the lost tooth and a pinch of tobacco, close both in mud (when it was warm) or snow (when it was cold), and throw it to the east so a new tooth would grow in its place. I wish I had honored this custom, because I got locked into Tooth Fairy duty with our first kid, and with eight more kids after her, it cost us a lot of money over the years.

The Ojibwe have long made dolls for their babies. In some places makers intentionally didn't put faces on the dolls—a teaching that emerged from former times when children normally only saw their reflections in the water. Dolls are a symbolic "reflection" of the child, and keeping them faceless was a reminder for children to think of themselves as spirits inside bodies rather than the bodies they saw in the water from time to time. Dolls with faces encourage focus on the physical part of being human, rather than the spiritual. My kids had every kind of doll, Power Ranger, and Teenage Mutant Ninja Turtle action figure you could imagine, so I never presented the faceless doll tradition as dogma with my crew. But as part of our cultural patrimony, it makes perfect sense to me. Ojibwe artist Jonathan Thunder illustrated *Gaa-pi-izhiwebak*, one of our Ojibwe language books, with stunning art inspired by faceless dolls.

Children are encouraged to wear moccasins or go barefoot. Their contact with the earth greets and connects to good spirits all around us. Wearing rubber or synthetic shoes is like wearing gloves when shaking hands with people. It's less intimate and seems untrusting. It's a good lesson for adults, too.

SPRING HARVEST

Food is central to every culture, and the Ojibwe are no exception. In addition to the expected ways that food defines a culture with a shared array of tastes and practices, the Indigenous food world is intertwined with our very indigeneity. Food control is people control. The US government encouraged the killing of sixty million buffalo by white settlers and professional hunters to starve the Plains tribes into submission. A sovereign nation is an independent one. For Ojibwe people, this means that harvesting our traditional foods and being self-reliant are connected and important to identity.

The precontact Ojibwe diet probably sounds bland to most people. Most of the food was eaten fresh or dried and rehydrated. Meats were boiled or roasted, never fried. The Ojibwe used few spices except for salt, and that in limited quantities. There are salt deposits in various places around the Great Lakes, but most are belowground, and salt just wasn't prized enough to be a major trade item. The Ojibwe did use maple sugar to season wild rice and meats. They also smoked a lot of meats to cure them for storage.

However, the Ojibwe diet is one of the healthiest in the world. Wild rice and blueberries, Ojibwe staples, are both superfoods. Ojibwe country holds an abundance of small and big game; many kinds of berries, mushrooms, tubers, and nuts; and some of the best fisheries on the planet. Between the abundant forage foods, fish, and game, the Ojibwe diet is balanced, nutrient rich, and varied enough to be quite stable in spite of the harsh climate. The Ojibwe also farmed corn, beans, and squash in many areas on the southern and eastern edges of Ojibwe country.

Today the Ojibwe are dealing with a host of health issues related to the abandonment of our precontact diet. Many people eat a lot of fried and highly processed foods, loaded with sugar and unhealthy fats and low in nutrients. Diabetes is common, shaving years off people's lives and quality off the final years for many. Many Ojibwe people need to get their gallbladders removed because their bodies have so much more difficulty digesting the foods we now eat. Cancers are common.

I have adopted the view that food is medicine and that our ancestors knew something about food. I was amazed when I was doing research for my book *Warrior Nation: A History of the Red Lake Ojibwe* to find how many people at Red Lake in the 1800s and early 1900s lived well into their nineties and past one hundred. And that was before the area had smallpox immunizations, ambulances, or hospitals. I'd love to say that my family gets most of its food off the grid—from the lakes and the woods. But the truth is that we get a lot of it from the grocery store or by going out to eat. We are growing this part of our life, though, and the effects on everyone's health and cultural vibrancy are obvious to me.

In addition to the benefits of consuming healthier food harvested in a respectful way, getting your food directly is a lifestyle choice. Hunting, fishing, and foraging, cutting firewood, and hauling maple sap are a perfect physical fitness regimen. They work the cardiovascular system as well as build muscle strength and bone density.

Every spring we go to the sugarbush where my babies' placentas are buried. We have a little ceremony and open the sugarbush with a prayer. And one of the kids shares the story of the sugarbush.

Long ago a man was stumbling through the woods, gaunt and weak with hunger. It was springtime in the north woods, and the ground was covered with deep snow. He tripped and fell. Fearing that he wouldn't have the strength to rise to his feet, he looked up and saw a misaabe (sasquatch) standing over him with a giant knife in his hand. The misaabe raised the knife as if to strike, and the man put his head down. He heard the misaabe swiftly bring the knife down but felt no blow. He looked up again, and where the misaabe had been standing was a giant maple tree with a gash in its trunk. He reached up with his hand and caught some of the life fluid bleeding from the tree. Bringing it to his mouth, he received a jolt of energy and rose to his feet. The fluid was pure maple syrup, and he returned to his village to share the gift with the people.

When we open the sugarbush we always mention the misaabe as one of the spirits who live in our area and help us through hard times. The maple tree we call ininaatig. It literally means "man tree" and refers to the misaabe (manlike creature) who turned into the tree. It's the tree of life.

I share another story about the maple harvest with my kids at this time. In this one, Wenabozho was checking up on the people. Wenabozho had power like a spirit but a personality like other Anishinaabeg, which means that he made mistakes and had ego issues like the rest of us. Wenabozho loved to receive offerings of tobacco and food. He was dismayed one spring to see the people harvesting maple syrup without offering tobacco to each of the trees or properly appreciating their harvest. Wenabozho started to drink tea. He drank many cups, pot after pot. Then, when the people weren't looking, he ran all over the sugarbush and peed by all the trees. It diluted the syrup coming out of the trees. Now, instead of pure maple syrup, the trees produced watery sap. The people had to work hard to cook the sap down into syrup or sugar. And they never took the trees for granted again. We offer tobacco to each tree when we tap it. In former times, tapping was done by cutting a gore into the tree and literally tapping another piece of wood into it. Some people used an open concave piece of wood just a few inches long. Others used a hollowed-out piece of wood, usually sumac, which has a hollow core. Today, most maple harvesters use a metal drill bit (7/16 inch is the standard size for maple taps) to make holes for setting taps, and most people use either metal or plastic taps. Some people hang bags right on the taps on the side of the trees, and others use tubing so the sap flows into buckets. In the spring, when the temperatures rise above freezing, maple sap begins to run up the trunk of each tree in preparation for making buds. When the temperature cools below freezing, it retreats back down the trunk. This flow of sap up and down the trunk is the maple run, and each tap collects a small dribble of sap, which flows down the tap and into a waiting bucket. My family uses two adjacent plots of land and alternates the harvest each year between them, so the trees get a rest. We haul the sap to the house and process it there. In former times, the Ojibwe moved the village to the sugarbush in the spring. But I use a truck and three-hundred-gallon tanks on a trailer to haul the sap.

Once we get the sap home, we cook it on an open fire outside. It takes anywhere from twenty-five to forty gallons of sap to produce one gallon of syrup. If we tried to boil it in the house, all the wallpaper would come off the walls from the massive evaporation effort. We hired a welder to make us a fifty-gallon metal pan and put it on top of a cut-down fuel-oil drum, lined with fire bricks. We burn wood inside the drum and vent the smoke through a metal chimney. It's a homemade contraption, but it works like a charm. Lots of other people have similar setups. My ancestors cooked everything down to sugar because it was easier to store and lasted longer; the Ojibwe didn't have canning jars until the 1900s. Nowadays, we mostly make syrup, but we cook some down to sugar and pour it into molds as well. The whole family gathers to haul sap, split firewood, and sit around the boiler when we cook the sap down to syrup.

My kids calculate the retail value of each year's harvest for fun, but we never sell our syrup. We share it around the whole extended family and gift some. We also use it in coffee and tea, on cereal, in oatmeal, and of course on pancakes and cheese blintzes.

For those who don't live in a rural area with plenty of maple

Caleb and Evan (back) watch Madeline tap a maple tree. ***Anton Treuer***

Boiling sap. From left: Anton Treuer, Margaret Treuer, Robert Treuer, Evan Treuer, Caleb Treuer, Luella Treuer, Elias Treuer, Blair Treuer, Margret Krueger.
Anton Treuer

trees, there are still many ways to participate in the maple harvest. A lot of people have small operations in urban areas. The maple is a common tree in places such as Milwaukee, Duluth, and Minneapolis, and a few taps in a couple yard trees is all it takes to get a taste of Ojibwe culture. For small operations like that, most people just cook the sap down in a big pot on a turkey fryer in the yard. Porky White, an Ojibwe elder from Leech Lake, maintained a large sugarbush operation in Maple Plain, in the greater Twin Cities area. After he passed away in 2001, his wife and friends kept his sugar camp going. Today, it's a community operation with hundreds of taps and many volunteers. There are chores in abundance there, and the good company of many people, who range from lifelong Ojibwe harvesters to beginners, participating in the maple harvest every spring. Check out the Facebook page for Porky's Sugarbush to get connected.

We conduct our spring maple harvest while listening to the woods. Something remarkable happens every spring. The first frogs start to sing, and that signals the end of the maple run. On the very same day they start singing, the sap starts to get cloudy and moths appear in the buckets. If the taps are left in after that, the sap will be sour, and it will hurt the trees. So, we always listen for the frogs. It's not simply the easiest way to know when to pull taps; the frog counts the seasons of winter on his hand. He has five fingers, just like us, and counts November, December, January, February, and March. He's quiet during those months. But when he awakens, he is calling in new life. It starts a spiritual cycle of rejuvenation and renewal. We are part of the web of life, not its masters, so we listen and follow the rhythm of nature with all we do.

The Mississippi River runs right by our house, and every species of fish comes by to spawn. The fish are protected during the spawn here except for brown suckers. My kids all put on hip waders and grab spears to harvest the suckers. They smoke well and make for good spring and summer meals.

When the ice retreats from the big lakes, a lot of Ojibwe people set nets or spear many species of fish. In some parts of Ojibwe country, this is done at night by light. In former times, people used birchbark torches with pine resin; today people use battery-powered lights. The male fish aggregate and swim around to fertilize the eggs laid in beds by the females. Over 85 percent of the fish harvested this way are male fish, reducing the impact on the population. That stands in contrast to angling, which takes male and female fish in equal numbers; since the females are larger in most fish species, those are kept more often, doing more harm to fish populations because of the means of harvest as well as the volume of the non-Native angler harvest.

SPRING CULTURE

There are ceremonies for every season. When the ice retreats from the lakes and rivers, we have our spring water ceremonies. While other families have their own ways of doing this, we make a miniature raft for each member of my family out of willow sticks. We mark them with green and red marks and tie the sticks together with yarn. Each member of our family places an item of used clothing on his or her raft—usually something small, such as a sock or T-shirt—along with tobacco. (Some people use a coin for each raft and a piece of maple sugar candy.) Then we float the rafts out in the river by our house. The offerings are for protection. It's a way of asking the spirits to take the offerings and not to take any family members while we are out and about on the waterways.

When the thunderbirds return, we hear the first thunders of spring. That's when we harvest the red willow. It's a common brush, also known as red osier dogwood, that grows all over Minnesota swamps and riverbanks. At this time of the year, the outer bark is

Evan reaches through red willow branches with a handful of tobacco.
Anton Treuer

paper thin. We sometimes run a fingernail down the length of the red willow sapling and then twist with both hands and the outer red bark pops right off. Then we use a butter knife to scrape down the next layer of bark. We save and dry that inner layer, either in the sun or in a quick and carefully monitored session in the oven. We then crush it and use it for tobacco. I prefer this for my own offerings. It is not the same as the Virginia leaf tobacco that gets processed into store-bought pipe and cigarette tobacco, but in the Ojibwe world, this is our tobacco. I think using tobacco that we harvest ourselves is spiritually stronger. We have made offerings for the harvest, rather than paid a company for it. Putting our hands on the production of tobacco this way gives it more value as an offering. There's a parallel with firewood: people who cut and split their own firewood burn it differently because of the sweat equity they put into it. Also, this kind of tobacco isn't loaded with numerous chemicals that kill you if you smoke it. Furthermore, schools and other organizations can use it without violating their tobacco policies or the Clean Indoor Air Act. The decolonized tobacco is the tobacco for me. And as a spiritual leader, I encourage others to make and use it, too.

I used to sit with Archie and work on red willow sticks to make tobacco. An old Ho-Chunk (Winnebago) man named Jim Funmaker used to visit Archie. Funmaker grew Ho-Chunk leaf tobacco in his garden, and there is a ceremony to the gardening of tobacco in the Ho-Chunk custom. Funmaker would show up with a couple garbage bags full of tobacco leaves. Archie and I would be waiting with garbage bags full of red willow tobacco. They traded even up—one bag of red willow for one bag of leaf tobacco. Then we sat in a circle and both of them mixed their leaf and red willow tobacco together in equal quantities. The new mixture is called geniginig in Ojibwe, and that where the word *kinnikinnick* comes from.

Our spring harvests—tobacco, fish, and maple—and the ceremonies around them always leave me full of hope and happiness. And the blessings of a big family and many children and grandchildren in this phase of their lives fill me with gratitude and wonder: gratitude for the cultural patrimony we have received, and wonder for what the next seasons have in store for all of them.

Isaac Treuer. ***Nedahness Greene***

SUMMER
Coming of Age

OJIBWE SUMMERS are characteristically hot and intense. They warm and nourish the natural world, and sometimes they light it on fire. This is the season of growing and maturing, coming of age, and finding purpose. It's a season that tests people like no other, but it also shows us who we are.

Of all my children, none exemplifies the trials and triumphs of this season better than my son Isaac. Mischievous and hilarious, intensely physical, uncommonly handsome, impulsive, and sometimes hot-tempered, he was a test all by himself throughout childhood. When he was two, he pushed his one-year-old brother, who was just starting to toddle. Isaac just looked at me and said, "I take time-out." I saved all his discipline reports, including from his early childhood program. They were numerous, and I intend to read as many as I can at his wedding reception someday. One (from his preschool) reads, "Today your son said some derivation of the word 'butt' at least 300 times—butt, buttocks, butt crack, butthole. Help!" Another from that year reads, "Today your son said a foul word in class. We informed him that this was not acceptable and that we had to tell his father to which he replied, 'You better not. I'll kick your ass. I'm a Power Ranger.'"

At age twelve he was punking out his little siblings. He had a special gift with the kind of mental torture that would get them crying without his touching them, so as not to invoke the harshest punishment from me. One day we were getting ready to load into the car and go to a drum ceremony, so I told him that if he didn't quit, I'd leave him home alone for the day. He gave them one more prod, so I left him and took the rest of the kids to drum. About an hour later he burst through the door to drum hall with beads of sweat on his forehead and a big grin across his face. He swaggered over to us. I had to ask, "How did you get here? Did you hitchhike?"

"No. I ran."

It was nine miles from our house to the dance hall. I didn't know whether I should be mad or proud. I was tempted to tell him that if he could get himself to the dance hall, he could get himself home again, too—but he would have taken that run again, with pleasure. He was impossible to discipline.

Isaac naturally commanded attention, but not all of the attention was good. He could provoke people. But his dark skin and long braids made him stand out to everyone from police officers to peers in unfair ways, as well, and he paid a heavy price for it at times. In former times, he simply would have been the most promising young warrior in the village. But in this day and age, he was a target, too.

Isaac is a natural in the woods. Even as a kid, he had great instincts for hunting and seemed to know exactly when to move and when to stand perfectly still. I started him out snaring rabbits. He could set snares with no snow on the ground and make kills consistently. Some of his skill just couldn't be taught. He was twelve when he got his first deer. We were in a little pop-up blind and spotted a couple deer two hundred yards out. The grass was so tall that he could barely see them. We watched for about twenty minutes as they slowly grazed a little closer. They were 130 yards out and the sun was starting to set. I thought it was a dicey shot for a kid trying to make his first kill, but Isaac said he would make it. As usual, I saw no point in arguing with him. He lined up, slowly exhaled and held, and then gently squeezed the trigger. The buck dropped immediately.

He was exhilarated but never lost his cool. He put tobacco down by the head of the deer and talked to the animal, explaining that he was hunting for food and that he wouldn't waste anything. He placed the deer's liver in a patch of hazel brush as an offering and hung the gonads next to it with another tobacco offering, this time to the Creator and helping spirits to watch over the deer nation that they may stay strong and plentiful.

Once we got his deer home and butchered, we started calling namesakes. A few weeks later, all of his namesakes, uncles, aunts, and grandparents descended on our house for his first kill feast. We cooked a venison roast and also fried up some of the loins, along with a host of other traditional Ojibwe foods—wild rice, berries, squash. We shared tobacco with all of the people gathered and said a prayer. Then, instead of eating, Isaac kneeled on the floor in front of Blair, who held up a spoon of the venison and said his Ojibwe name, Bezhigo-bines (Lone Thunderbird). He refused the first bite of food, saying, "No, I am thinking of children who don't have enough to eat." Some of those in attendance looked at one another and then nodded their heads in affirmation. Blair took a new spoonful of the venison and offered it to him a second

Isaac's first kill. ***Anton Treuer***

time. He refused again, saying, "No, I am thinking of my elders who cannot get out into the woods to hunt for themselves." There were more nods and all eyes on Isaac. Blair offered him a bite of the venison for a third time. Again, he refused. "No, I am thinking of my family and the people who came here today to support me." She offered him a bite of venison for the fourth time, and this time he ate.

Then the teachings began. All of the successful hunters in the room imparted wisdom to him. We explained: "Up until today you were what we called a dependent. You depended on all the people in this room to provide all of your food. But today, you provide for all of us. This is what it means to be an adult. From today forward you will have a special gift—the ability to gather resources. You will exercise this ability every time you hunt, fish, or gather, and every time you work at a job. Use your ability to take care of children who don't have enough, elders who can't get it for themselves, your family, and your community. This is what it means to be an adult." He was made to give away the rest of his kill—packaged up and frozen venison. His namesakes gave him hunting knives and tobacco pouches, new gloves and a set of long underwear.

While no kind of discipline ever seemed to get through to my son, his first kill feast was truly transformative. Isaac internalized that set of teachings and applied it over and over throughout his maturation to adulthood. It was amazing for me to see, especially since it seemed like I didn't need to remind him about those teachings after that.

One time a friend of mine was complaining about his back and how hard it was for him to get out in the woods and hunt. Isaac was sixteen then. He didn't say a word. But he went out in the woods and harvested a deer, dragged it home, processed it, tanned the hide, and then drove over to my friend's house and filled up his freezer—and gave him the tanned hide. My friend was on the edge of tears, saying, "I didn't know people even remembered that custom."

Later that spring, Isaac had a friend who wanted to go to prom. His friend's mother kept promising to help him get a tux, but she just didn't have the money. They missed the deadline to order one, and his friend—heartbroken—prepared to cancel his prom date. Isaac, without telling anyone, took his friend to the Goodwill and found a used tux that fit and bought it for him with his own money.

We can say that Ojibwe culture is communal. We can say that we are generous. But those are just words. The first kill ceremony planted those teachings in my son. Our cultural toolbox reflects the values of the Ojibwe people, but it shapes the values of our people in equal measure.

School was a challenge for Isaac. The problems weren't academic for him; they were cultural. Isaac could sit in a deer stand for five hours without flinching, but he couldn't sit at a desk for five minutes. He was hard on his teachers, and sometimes they reciprocated. The schools always stressed about standardized tests. They sent letters home for weeks to make sure the kids were there, on time, well fed, well rested, and well medicated. Isaac was about five minutes into one of his three-hour fifth-grade standardized tests when he stood up and yelled, "Finished! I'm finished! Are you finished?" Blair and I were in the special education office soon after to discuss an individualized education plan (IEP).

When I think about the attributes of mainstream white American culture I think of individualism, materialism, and competition. How many board games or sports are not about winning? The connections were obvious to me as we started looking at the toolbox for Isaac's IEP: "You have a wonderful and strong-spirited son here. We value him and want to catch him being good. If he's good, his card stays green. If he slips, he drops to purple, blue, yellow, orange, red. But he can climb back up through the rainbow anytime, too. Can you sign this permission slip so we can give him gum? If he stays green long enough, he can get some gum. We'll work a chart of gold stickers. When he gets enough, he can get a treat from the treat box." Everything was about rewards and punishments. That's the school-age equivalent of materialism—competing for more stickers, card flips, treats, and gum.

I had to tell them that this kid was completely unmotivated by rewards and punishments. I had tried that. It didn't work. He could do any punishment standing on his head with a smile—it just didn't motivate him. But he was highly motivated by relationships.

To the credit of the education team, they listened. We worked out a plan that focused on relationships. We set him up to tell stories to kids a couple grades younger than him. We had him lead groups to gym class. There were plenty more challenges. But by the time he was eighteen, Isaac graduated from high school, staying in mainstream classrooms with good grades, no medications, and undiminished swagger and enthusiasm for life. That's the power of connecting with someone in their cultural language.

FIRST KILL

The preceding description of Isaac's first kill experience gives you the critical information you need on that milestone ceremony. Both boys and girls get first kill feasts when they become successful hunters. The girls in our crew hunt as avidly and as skillfully as the boys. When we do the first kill feasts, we do often describe unique challenges and responsibilities for men and women.

There are four primary kinds of deer: fawns, does, immature bucks, and mature bucks. Male and female fawns act much the same way. Young and mature does act the same way as one another, too. But there are differences between immature and mature bucks. We often tell successful hunters to pay close attention to the different kinds of deer. For Isaac, that meant paying close attention to male deer. The most dangerous deer in the woods is actually not a large, mature, big-antlered buck. The deer most likely to charge someone is an immature buck with just two or four points on his rack. The immature bucks don't get to breed because they are chased off by the larger bucks. But they are full of pheromones and adrenaline. They are often impulsive, aggressive, and athletic. They make the most mistakes. And they pay the highest price. Of all the deer in the woods, they are the kind most likely to get shot. A mature buck has lived through a few hunting seasons. He knows to stay in the swamps and move at night more than during the day. He moves more slowly, listening, smelling, and circling. They are different creatures.

The difference between immature and mature bucks provides a perfect metaphor for manhood. Young men, like young bucks, are full of hormones, energy, adrenaline. They are more impulsive and less cautious. They are athletic and treated with more suspicion and disregard. They often act before they think. And of all humans on the planet, young men can least afford to make mistakes, and they often pay the price when they do. They populate juvenile detention centers and jails and morgues. So, the advice to young men is to *think of who they are and who they want to be*—to act like a mature buck in order to become one.

Young women receive teachings from these descriptions, too. Those teachings show them how does survive the hunters, help their fawns live through their first fall and winter, and navigate the different kinds of bucks sure to cross their paths.

I love the first kill feast for many reasons. It provides real wisdom. It instills teachings and values in young people. It engages their namesakes and extended family in empowering ways. The young hunters feel pride and identify with our traditions and their ancestors. At the ceremony, before we eat, the successful hunter shares the story of their kill. They transition from passive listeners to tellers of story—from observers to carriers of tradition.

BECOMING A WOMAN

The transition to adulthood manifests itself in many different but intersecting ways—physical, emotional, spiritual, and cultural. Customarily, when a girl's body begins to change, her mother, aunts, grandmothers, and female namesakes are made aware. The girl anticipates and prepares. When she gets her first menstrual period, a year of ceremonies and cultural protocols follows, usually directed by the women in the girl's life. There is a lot of variation in these customs across Ojibwe country.

A girl's first year transitioning to womanhood is considered an especially sacred time. Her monthly periods are physical demonstrations of her power to bring life into the world, but throughout the year, she is surging with this positive spiritual energy. Her power is great during this time, and she is instructed to be careful with it. When we push two magnets together, they will repel one another, even though neither magnet's power is considered bad. So, a girl is told that her power can impact other spiritual forces around her. In former times, a girl was often sequestered for her first menstrual period and kept a distance from many ceremonies, and even from men, as much as was practical, for her entire first year. I know some families that still do a sequester, bringing the girl food in her bedroom and limiting her time in shared space with other members of the house. We did not do a full sequester with our daughters, but we did keep the girls primarily in female space and away from ceremonies during this time.

As each of our daughters entered womanhood, she received her own set of dishes, and for a year she ate her food off those dishes unless we were out to eat at a restaurant. This practice was accompanied by numerous affirmations of her positive spiritual power and was received as an exercise in empowerment. Some families have their girls in transition refrain from eating all forms of berries for one year; at the conclusion of the year, they are fed berries at a special feast. In our family, we had our daughters refrain from eating all traditional Ojibwe foods harvested after the start of her transition year until they could be feasted. One at a time, as they came into season, we had a feast for our daughters with a ritual feeding similar to the one at the first kill feast—four offerings of the food, with the first three refused. If a girl got her first period in the spring, we would feast the maple syrup with her in March, fresh-caught fish in April, then berries in June, wild rice in September, and freshly harvested game in November. At each feast, we explained how her great power as a woman could even push away a hunter's luck or the flow of energy to a berry crop.

Some of the first-year taboos were really difficult. Our daughters refrained from touching all forms of new life—puppies and babies. Our oldest daughter went through this experience when one of our other daughters was born and waited to hold and handle her until her year was complete. Even swimming in lakes and rivers where there was wild rice growing or where people fished was off-limits. In former times people washed up at nonfishing lakes or with wash basins or tubs. We were at a summer camp one year when one of our daughters got her first period. She was distraught, so I called her namesakes to see whether there was an exception for special conditions. Dora Ammann, one of Archie's daughters and namesake to my girls, responded, "No exceptions. It will be hard now. But she will remember this. And she will grow up with a deeper understanding of her innate feminine power. She will respect herself more this way." We stuck to our protocol, and that's exactly what happened.

For their entire first year as a woman, our daughters stayed away from major ceremonies and wore gloves if they had to touch personal ceremony items. They used cedar to make tea and use as a wash. They were told not to step over anyone's personal items. I have nine kids, and the front doorway was usually piled with boots, coats, mittens, and hats. The girls didn't have to stand in the cold at times like this. They just yelled at their brothers, "You guys better come get your crap out of my way or I'm gonna whammy you!" If the boys were slow to respond, they just gave the boy stuff a swift kick and sent it flying and marched right in.

At the end of each girl's first year as a woman there was a big feast. Everyone in the family attended. The female namesakes and adult women in the family usually ran the show. We made a tobacco and food offering. If the young woman hadn't yet been fed her final traditional food, we did it at this feast. Then all of the women started sharing formal teachings. They had been sharing teachings informally all year, but this was now being done publicly. They told her that if she ever saw a group of women sitting around and visiting, she should come join them and sit down, because she was a woman now. They told her that at ceremonies, there were special jobs for women and for men. The two gender energies live in balance. Women have spiritual dominion over the water. Women carry their babies in water in the womb. Their energy and emotions flow like water. The moon is a female spirit that pulls at the water on earth, creating tides. When she gets her monthly period, it is a visit from grandmother moon. They told our daughters that wearing a skirt is a way to demonstrate their affirming identification as women. It is not, as has often been the case in other cultures, a way to keep women in an inferior position to men.

They told our daughters that they have a right and a responsibility to be respected by men. They explained that this meant that nobody could hit them. Nobody could call them names. Nobody could make them do something sexually that they did not want to do. I truly believe that if everyone gave these teachings to their girls as they became women, this world would be a different place. And if we gave all these teachings to our young women with their brothers watching, this world would be a different place even faster.

BECOMING A MAN

The key physical change for boys becoming men is the change of their voice. First kill feasts impart a lot of teachings about adulthood, but both boys and girls hunt and receive those teachings. Often there are gender-specific teachings given as part of that ceremony, too, and these are extremely powerful. Boys receive additional cultural instruction in two ways: participation in warrior activities and fasting.

Warrior activities are not about waging war. These are meetings and activities where men gather to share their experiences and teachings about manhood. In former times, these were much more structured. Boys becoming men had to earn the right to wear certain kinds of war paint by deeds of service or valor. They acquired the right to keep the claws of birds and paws of animals—crow, hawk, coyote, wolf, and bear—over time and by winning the approval of adult males in the group for their sustained acts of service. That service could range from stacking the firewood at grandma's house without being told to getting a job and helping to support the family to learning the use of weapons and protecting the village. Men would keep warrior bundles, collections of sacred items for spiritual protection. Today, some of these customs have eroded or changed. But I made a point of helping my sons develop bundles and getting them bear claws for protection. Their namesakes and other men in our circle come over and meet at least four times a year, sharing teachings and demonstrating by example the role and disposition of Ojibwe men.

Fasting is the other primary way in which boys receive instruction as men. Anyone can fast—boys, girls, men, and women. But fasting for a vision is especially emphasized for boys becoming men, and it is accompanied by special men's teachings. Here, too, there is variation in Ojibwe practices. Some people use a sweat lodge to purify people before they fast. Others drink a medicine boiled into tea the night before they start their fast. Some people fast in a platform in a tree about six feet off the ground. Others fast sitting right on the ground. Some people smoke a pipe while fasting, and others prohibit anything touching the mouth.

I follow the protocol given to me for my first fasts: cleansing by a medicine that is drunk in tea form the night before the fast and fasting in a platform in a tree. When I put my sons out fasting, I had them place an eagle feather on the roof of the house above the door. The spirits find us when we sleep to bring us dreams. When those spirits saw the feather, they knew my sons were in the woods rather than the house.

Sometimes people declare before they go out that they will fast for a certain number of days. I usually have people fast until they get a vision. It might take one day, four days, or more. There are cautionary tales about fasting. In one, a man fasted for a long time and eventually transformed into the shape of a robin; he could never be human again. He tried to fly around his family, but he had to go south for the winter. They never saw him again. In the book *Akawe Niwii-tibaajim*, Ralph Pewaush tells a cautionary tale about a man who was fasting and received the blessings of spirits in the trees. But he didn't pay attention to what he was being gifted, didn't see what he had received, and he fasted even longer. He eventually came in from his fast, but he was permanently bonded with the forest. In the autumn, the leaves changed colors, and the man sickened. The leaves fell, and he died. Because of these cautionary teachings, we always have someone check each day on the person fasting. If they are spiritually, emotionally, or physically stretched to their limits, it is time to come in. And when I put people out, if they get a vision, they come in. Even the most experienced fasters should have someone be their host, who checks up on them and has the authority to take them in, even if the faster objects.

Isaac was remarkable on his fast. He was thirteen years old at the time. A lot of people struggle with being alone when they are fasting. Isaac grew up in a crowded house with constant social interaction with his siblings. Most people have at least some level of that, plus the constant chatter of televisions, the internet, and smartphones. He had his body and a blanket. No fire. No pipe. No company. No food or water. I told him that life would be this way at times for him as a man. Sometimes he would have to make decisions without consulting anyone. He would have to be self-reliant and mentally strong. I told him that he would have to turn off or tune out the human chatter in his life to be spiritually guided. Our physical sight gets in the way of our spiritual sight.

I told him that there was life all around all the time that he had never noticed. Every day he had been stepping over insects and moving too fast to notice the birds and animals watching him. I said that it might take a couple days before his body purged the toxins from the food and human environment and his body would be unhappy with him while it did. But when his body started to shut down, his spirit would awaken. This was the time to pay attention to the natural world and the spirit world.

Isaac was so tough. Once each day, before sunset, I went to check on him. If he had not yet had a vision, he would sit for another day. I looked for signs of physical and mental stress when I checked on him. Day one, no vision. I asked whether anything was hard—going without food and water, anything else. He looked worn but said, "No." Day two. "No." Day three. "No." He never complained once about hunger, cold, thirst. He did say, "I notice how loud the woods are. There are so many animals and birds. There is something happening all day every day. And then, at the very end of the day every day, the wind stops. The birds quit singing. The woods are perfectly still. It feels like somebody died. Then, a few minutes later, the nighttime birds and animals start to move and make different noises."

I was amazed by his observations. We have teachings in the Ojibwe world that daytime is nighttime for the spirits of the deceased, and vice versa. But I had never told him about this. We even have a taboo about whistling at night. A whistle is a call in Ojibwe culture, and calling to the dead might invite them to call back. It could invoke a tug at someone's spirit to enter the spirit world. So, it's taboo. Isaac never knew the depth of all this, but he could intuit it on his fast.

Some people refrain from eating certain birds and animals from birth until after they have fasted just in case one of them is meant to reveal itself in a vision years later. Turtle, bear, and other creatures are especially sacred, and while they make good table fare, they often help Anishinaabeg in spiritual ways, too. Once someone has had a vision and knows which spirits have established a guardianship over them, the rest are fine eating.

Isaac's patience, strength, and intuition paid off. He looked a little leaner when I came to check on him on his fourth day, but he was smiling. Hard-earned success. I told him to keep his vision to himself. It was personal empowerment meant for him, not for me. If he needed to share his gifts with others, he would know when and how. After that, Isaac seemed to walk a little slower, look at things just a little longer. He exuded a quiet confidence underneath his normal extroverted intensity. He deepened and matured.

BECOMING A PIPE CARRIER

In my world, someone can earn the right to carry a ceremonial pipe in many ways. Someone can dream of a pipe and make it. Someone else can gift a pipe to someone, and the receiving comes with the right and responsibility to care for and use the pipe. After a successful fast, often people make or receive a pipe. It's a tool to deepen their spiritual intuition. It's used to transform offerings of tobacco into a smoke form and send them along with one's thoughts and prayers. It amplifies one's thoughts and prayers and comes with solemn responsibility. People who are seated on ceremonial drums or initiated into the medicine dance are automatically qualified to be pipe carriers as well.

Once someone becomes a pipe carrier, they are expected to respect, care for, and use their pipe. They are not merely owners but carriers. They carry the pipe for the benefit of others. If someone passes tobacco to a pipe carrier and asks them to help at a ceremony or pray for them, such requests are normally granted without protest.

Pipes consist of a bowl, a stem, and a bag. There are many variations in pipe style and materials. Hardwoods are practical for longevity of the stem and have medicinal qualities. But cedar and sumac are easier to work and preferred in some areas. Both of those are medicinal, too. Some pipe bowls are made of white or rose quartz and considered to have healing power. Red catlinite bowls are well known and common in Ojibwe country. The red stone comes from quarries at Rice Lake (Wisconsin), Lac Courte Oreilles (Wisconsin), and Pipestone (Minnesota). Only Pipestone is open to the public, and that has been contested by some Native people who really want the red stone available for tribal people for prayer pipes rather than for manufacture as tourist trinkets for non-Natives. A lot of Ojibwe also use black stone for their pipes. Most of the black stone comes from under the water and is harvestable only at certain times of the year. The Canadian Shield around Rainy Lake and Lake of the Woods has big black stone deposits, but they are not shared publicly. The red stone is associated with earth spirits. The black stone is associated with water spirits.

Pipes aren't kept in boxes, although they can be wrapped in cloth if someone does not yet have a proper pipe bag. The bowl is often wrapped in cloth when not in use so it doesn't touch the stem, which activates its connection and power. My pipe bag has separate pouches for the bowl and the stem.

SWEAT LODGE

There are many kinds of sweat lodge ceremony in our area. Each has its own story and practice. These are personal to the keeper of each lodge, so I won't give details, but in general, a sweat lodge is made by bending saplings and tying them to one another, then covering them with bark, blankets, or tarps. Rocks are heated on a fire outside the lodge and brought inside, where water or medicine is poured on them. It's dark, hot, and sweaty. The ceremony is used to purify and heal participants, who usually take turns singing and praying. Sometimes medicines are burned on the rocks or poured over them in tea form. Sweat lodges are not saunas, though. They are used for purification and prayer.

I keep a sweat lodge on our family property. My siblings and I gather there with our children so we can all pray together and purge some of the stresses and hard times. Many sweat lodges are open to people of all ages, although children usually don't need the ceremony as often because they are usually healthier and have fewer emotional burdens than the adults (though not always). When we do a family sweat, it is men, women, and children doing the ceremony together. But it's also common for a group of men or women to have segregated ceremonies. The gender affinity space helps some people unload emotional burdens and traumas.

Sweat lodges are widely practiced. When I lived in Milwaukee, the American Indian Center there regularly held sweat lodge ceremonies. The same is true for a number of Native organizations in the Twin Cities, Duluth, and other places. For those looking to find a ceremony like this, reach out to the Native organizations near you. They'll be glad to help.

MEDICINES

The Ojibwe world is full of medicine, and we use it in many ways. Sage is dried on the stalk and then typically stripped before use, rolled into a ball, and burned in a small dish or abalone shell. It purifies the space spiritually. Sometimes people place other medicines on top of the burning sage ball. Cedar and sweetgrass are also commonly used this way. In English, this is usually called smudging. We have many other medicines that we boil into tea form for drinking. Others are eaten. Some are applied topically to the skin for rashes and other ailments. Application methods vary, and there are thousands of traditional medicines.

My daughter Madeline used to have chronic ear infections. We had many miserable nights and trips to the doctor over the years. I finally brought her to a medicine man who told us that the problem wasn't her ears. He said that a node behind her ears—the mastoid—was getting infected, and it was putting pressure on her ears. He gave her a medicine and did a ceremony to direct it to kill the sickness in her mastoid. It worked. She never had another ear infection again after that. But the medicine he used can't just be taken without the ceremony; it is actually a toxin, and without being spiritually directed it could hurt someone. A lot of our medicines work like this. The science behind a plant and its medicinal properties must work hand in hand with the spiritual process. Without that, it's just academic. Academic understanding of ethnobotany tells us a lot about science—but not a lot about Ojibwe culture. It is the cultural use of the plants that makes them medicine in the Ojibwe world.

In the beginning of this book, I addressed the problem with using anthropological information in a book to experience Ojibwe culture. I feel much the same about providing ethnobotanical information in a book to teach about Ojibwe healing. It just doesn't work like that. Although I am mentioning certain

Caleb cuts lily pad root for medicine. ***Anton Treuer***

common medicines associated with some of our ceremonies, such as a baby's first bath, people who want to learn about the healing arts and sciences need to take tobacco and go to their healers for the details.

DEALING WITH THE DARK SIDE

Summer is a season of growth, maturation, and coming of age; but it is a season of many tests as well. For the survival of the human race, young people must transition from dependents to independent beings. They have to break with their parents. It's healthy and necessary. But a lot of things can get in the way. When a young person has experienced trauma or developed acute anxiety, they may fear separating from the parental bond and going their own way. Parents are humans, too, and for the same reasons, they sometimes cling to or try to control their kids. Negotiating this separation with healthy people can also go sideways. Some of us are wired with great intensity or passivity. We break hard or with drama, late or not at all. The lives of the parents and the maturing young person will necessarily be rearranged. There are always growing pains.

As young people become adults, their attachments with their guardians change, and they form new attachments. These new connections to people (friends, romantic partners) and places (college, new jobs, the homes of friends) can be healthy or unhealthy. Adjusting to the changes can be healthy or unhealthy.

There is a spirit in all things. Each human is capable of doing good or engaging in darkness. Things work the same way. Tobacco, when used as an offering, can be an instrument of good. When abused, it can cause cancer and kill you. Alcohol may have some attributes often viewed as positive in terms of health or social lubrication, but there is clearly a dark side to alcohol as well. It is addictive and destroys the bodies of many people. It causes errors of human judgment that shatter lives—car crashes, violent or irresponsible behavior. There are very few things and very few people that are obviously 100 percent good or 100 percent bad for you. It's both with most things in life.

Since I have raised many children and been down this road often, I have to say that the cultural toolbox is my best friend in navigating tough terrain. Since there is a spirit in all things, we should approach all things with a spiritual frame of mind—be mindful of the energy in things and people. With people, the best protection is being good to others. Usually, people reciprocate what's coming at them. Some do not respond to goodness with positivity, and that's when we need healthy boundaries and a strong sense of self. It's the same with things. We become who we hang out with. I tell my kids that if they want a spiritual life, they should hang out with good spirits—on a fast, in the woods, at our ceremonies, and at healthy social events. If they seek other people (imperfect though we all are) who are looking for those things, they will develop a spiritual path. If they hang out with people who are using and boozing, guess what happens? We need to feed the good and starve the bad the best way we can. That means setting boundaries with toxic people. It means creating distance from unhealthy things.

I have always told my kids that there are a thousand definitions of success and happiness. They don't need to pick mine. But they do need to pick one, and I will support them on their journey. One is a teacher. One is planning to go to medical school. One is an elder care assistant. One is going to an Ivy League college. One is working at a coffee shop while he tries to figure out which definition of success really speaks to him. It's all beautiful to me. I push back, express concern, or lean in when they violate their own integrity or self-stated goals. And I catch and support without rescuing as best I can when they stumble.

In the spring section, I shared the metaphor of the ax: when there is a bramble in someone's life, they should pick up their ax, meaning they should pick up their ways. The rituals of this phase of life normalize places, people, and practices they can use to stabilize and heal. As a result, young people—while they're prone to making mistakes and necessarily breaking from the parental bond—are equipped with community, extended family, and ceremony. They have an ax to get them through the brambles.

SUMMER HARVEST

Summer is a time of increasing abundance. My family works hard during the spring sugarbush, and the pantry is full of jars of syrup when we head into summer. We start fishing in the spring, too, but summer opens up angling and sport fishing. One of my sons enjoys it so much that he wants to be a professional fisherman. Our property has many kinds of berries and nuts. Wild strawberries are more scattered; they are a treat, but not a staple. But raspberries, chokecherries, plums, and blueberries are abundant and treasured. We also harvest hazelnuts in the late summer. The hazelnuts themselves are about half the size of the ones you'll find in most grocery stores. When it's harvest time, a layer of thick, leafy tissue covers each nut. The surface of the hull looks fuzzy, but it has a thin layer of sap, as sticky as sap from a pine tree. Picking the hazelnuts means pulling the entire bundle of sappy tissue off of the branch for each nut harvested. We usually wear gloves—otherwise it takes some work to get the sap off your hands. Then we dry out the nuts and hulls, which lose their moisture and separate from the nuts. We roast those with the shells on and then crack them open and snack away. They are delicious.

I bring the entire family with me when I travel to Archie's community, where I officiate ceremonies every summer. Even our adult kids usually attend. Away from home, we get a chance to focus on the ceremony, of course, but time with one another as well. Usually, we

Mia and I clean blueberries. ***Blair Treuer***

camp out at the ceremony grounds for two two-week ceremonies—one in June and another in August. It's a major commitment of our time. We build our summer harvest plans around it.

We garden, although we don't put out the kind of quantities we might if we weren't on the move so much for ceremonies. Summer brings abundant forage food as well. Morel mushrooms are highly prized and plentiful in the hardwoods. There are nineteen species of edible mushrooms in our area. There are some poisonous ones, too, so newcomers do need to study up a little before getting adventurous. Milkweed buds, when they are new in midsummer, are great table fare, but when they start getting fibrous in August, they can induce vomiting.

We harvest supplies in the summer months, too. In May and June, the basswood bark peels best. The inner bark is split and used for string. Sometimes we collect a couple garbage bags full for the construction of wigwams, sweat lodges, and baskets.

We manage our property with our harvest practices in mind. I often order trees and shrubs from the Minnesota State Forest Nursery, a program of the Minnesota Department of Natural Resources that's been selling seedlings in bulk since the 1930s. Some years we plant cedar, which we use for medicine, along the swamps and Mississippi River. Some years we plant chokecherry, plum, and pin cherry. In the DNR's wildlife packs we often get red willow (they call it red osier dogwood) and plant that, too, even though it's naturally abundant. Our ancestors used to shape the land in other ways. Sometimes they used fire to burn the underbrush for propagating blueberries. We have a few more tools and resources than they had, but it's the same idea.

SUMMER CULTURE

Like every group of people, Ojibwe people have changed a lot over time. In previous eras, we probably spent more of our time harvesting in the summer months, but for our crew, summer is also when the kids are not in school and I am not teaching at the university. Our whole family spends at least four weeks every summer camped out at the medicine dance grounds in Round Lake, Wisconsin. The rest of the time is split between harvesting, swimming, visiting, and fun cultural activities.

We join lots of other Ojibwe people at the powwows in our area. I would probably powwow even more if we weren't so busy with ceremonies, and I'll probably go more often as the kids keep flying the coop and my schedule eases up a little.

Powwows are a part of modern Ojibwe culture and the culture of many other tribes, but this wasn't always the case. Powwows themselves reflect both cultural continuity and change. Music and dance have always been part of Indigenous cultures. Sometime after 1862, the Ojibwe were given three different kinds of ceremonial drums by the Dakota as a peace offering between the tribes. These drums were the physical and spiritual center points of ceremonies, which were new at the time, and spread rapidly across the Great Lakes. Most Ojibwe communities in our area embraced them. Some attributes of the modern powwow evolved from this older, more religious use of the drum. The style of singing and dancing is different from other Ojibwe musical traditions. Several men sit at a drum, singing together; one individual sings a lead verse, all singers sing a second verse, and then all sing two verses (collectively called a pushup); and sometimes these are followed by a tail (one verse). All of these dimensions of the musical style transferred to the powwow that evolved out of older ceremonial drum dances in the early 1900s.

There are other tribal influences on the powwow. Some Plains tribes, in particular, had warrior and hunting traditions that transferred into the new Ojibwe powwow space. For example, successful hunters in some Plains tribes saved teeth from elk kills, and in one traditional dress style, a woman sews elk teeth all over the dress to signify that she is married to a successful hunter. That is stylized now—not all displayed elk teeth are from a spouse's kills. In Ojibwe war and politics, eagle feathers used to be earned, usually through military deeds. Men earned feathers for killing an enemy, being wounded in battle, and so forth. Civil chiefs used to display an otter-skin turban, and it was a special right for hereditary chiefs. Today, most of the male styles of dance display eagle feathers, and many people wear otter-skin turbans. The significance of these things has changed over time. Big feather war bonnets and eagle-feather bustles worn on the back of men's powwow regalia are also carryovers from Plains tribes that used to display feathers these ways as evidence of military deeds.

During the 1918 influenza pandemic (often called the Spanish flu), the Ojibwe people suffered many losses. Archie Mosay was eighteen years old then. In one night, his maternal grandmother, aunt, and two siblings died. During this trying time, an Ojibwe man had a dream about the jingle dress, a source of healing for the people through dance, and that became a distinct style of powwow regalia for women. It remains one of the most popular today.

There are six primary styles of dance at modern powwows. Men's traditional is a warrior style of dance. It's characterized by the display of eagle feathers in bustles on the back and on top of the head, either in a roach or in an otter-skin turban. We imitate the actions of warriors when we dance—hunting, tracking, charging. I dance men's traditional, as do most of my sons. The grass dance is another popular style of male dance. This is also a warrior dance, but instead of displaying eagle feathers on the back, the dancers have long, swaying fringe on their regalia and imitate the movements of hunters and warriors tracking game or enemies in the tall grass. Men's fancy dance is a stylized form of men's traditional that incorporates more acrobatic moves. Women's traditional is

Luella greets me at a Leech Lake powwow. ***Blair Treuer***

characterized by long, flowing fringe on long dresses. The movements are slower, regal, and dignified. Women's jingle dress is characterized by numerous metal jingles sewn onto the dresses and the swooshing sound to the dance style, which is more energetic. Women's fancy dance incorporates a shawl and fast, spinning dance moves in which the women imitate the motions of a butterfly coming out of its cocoon. There are other styles of dance, such as chicken dance, in which male dancers imitate the movements of prairie chickens, which are making their way into Ojibwe country now, too.

Since the early 1900s, powwows have also been influenced by non-Native customs. We now parade into the dance arena in a grand entry, by dance category, like entrants to a rodeo. We have evolved French social dances into the modern '49 dance—where everyone dances with a partner. It's a common feature in the evenings at many powwows. Powwows are social and open to everyone. You don't even need a powwow outfit to dance. There is an announcer who lets people know if there are any special songs during which only people of a certain dance category dance at a time.

Powwow is not nearly as ancient as a lot of our ceremonies, but that doesn't diminish its value. Our artistic and musical traditions are alive at powwows. Tens of thousands of Native people compose songs every year. Hundreds of thousands make powwow outfits. Ojibwe people have embraced the powwow and made it their own. It's cultural change, but it's cultural continuity, too. And powwow is fun, exciting, and a good, clean, sober place for people to gather. Often as many as five generations in one family dance together. And intergenerational participation in shared culture is powerful.

ART

There are many traditional Ojibwe art forms and many modern adaptations of them. Most of these are practiced every season of the year, although some materials are best harvested in the summer. Birchbark peels best in the early summer, and this is when people customarily made birchbark canoes and baskets. Once birchbark has dried, it's not as pliable, even when rehydrated. We also rebuild sweat lodges and wigwams for ceremonial use in the late spring and early summer; saplings bend well then. We manufacture string from the inner bark of basswood, and this is the season when it peels and separates the best. By fall, it's dry, brittle, and hard to manage. The freshly peeled basswood bark is called wiigoob, but once manufactured into string, it's called asigobaan. Sometimes we pull more than we need at the time, because unlike birchbark, the basswood fiber rehydrates easily for later use. Even in the winter, people rehydrate stored basswood to work on ash baskets.

The Ojibwe do not have many natural dyes in this area, but there are some. Indigo and vermilion can be used to develop blue and red dyes. Charcoal was often infused into pine pitch for the dark, black lines on canoes. We used to rely on moose hair and porcupine quills for embroidery, but once European trade beads came to the Great Lakes in the middle of the 1600s, older Ojibwe embroidery styles easily incorporated the new materials. Today, beadwork is everywhere. It's on pipe bags, bandolier bags, vests, purses, pouches, and of course powwow regalia. I have beadwork on my hat. My mom had it on her tennis shoes, and that made her a stylin' grandma and an object of envy everywhere she went.

Ojibwe beadwork often incorporates a floral style—lots of flowers, vines, blueberries, often stylized and brightly colored. Of course, the Ojibwe are inspired by everything in the natural world. Our area has a complex ecosystem and a rich variety of plant life.

Beadwork on display. From left: Babette Sandman, Monique Paulson, Dora Ammann, Anton Treuer. Connie Rivard of St. Croix, Wisconsin, made my bandolier bag; Travis DeBungee of Ponemah, Minnesota, made the others. ***Blair Treuer***

But it's more than that. In our creation story, all the plants were made and placed on earth before any sentient life. The floral beadwork and artistic pattern are a humble reminder of our place in the creation—one of dependence on the natural world and all its abundance, not the other way around.

The Ojibwe have created visual art since the start of the great migration—there are petroglyphs throughout the Great Lakes. Today, there are numerous visual artists who engage in this part of our culture in new ways. Rabbett Before Horses is a special favorite of mine, as are Carl Gawboy, Sam English, Patrick DesJarlait, and Joe Geshick. Some use paint, while others innovate in other genres. Sarah Howes has a clothing line and visual art business based in Fond du Lac that populates Ojibwe homes all over the United States and Canada.

GAMES AND PLAY

In former times, the Ojibwe worked incredibly hard throughout every season, but sports and games were always an important dimension of the culture. The Ojibwe loved lacrosse. My ancestral village is Bena, and the neighboring village is called Ball Club in English. In Ojibwe it's Baaga'adowaan, meaning "Lacrosse Pitch"—clearly where Ball Club came from. Historical references to the widespread function of lacrosse abound, both as a social part of culture and as a means of dispute resolution. And the Ojibwe often made major wagers over lacrosse competitions between villages or tribes.

We have stories still shared about famous lacrosse games, such as the one in 1763, during Pontiac's War, when the Ojibwe and Odawa staged a game with the Meskwaki at Fort Mackinac in Michigan. There were hundreds of players, and as the game progressed, British soldiers lined the walls of the fort to watch. Eventually, someone threw the ball over the wall of the fort. The soldiers opened the gate so the game could continue, and the Natives pulled out concealed weapons and took over the fort.

Initially lacrosse wasn't a human game. It was an epic contest between the four-legged animals and the birds. The animals were larger and more powerful, especially the moose, elk, and bear. They were overly proud and often refused to let the smaller animals play. The birds were smaller than the four-legged creatures, but fast and agile and clever. This contest was repeated over and over, until one year the large animals took for granted their advantages and made fun of the smallest animals among them—the bapashkwaanashiinh and the zhagaskaandawe. The birds saw an opportunity in this and invited these two little animals to join them. They agreed. The birds then started to pull on the bodies of the little animals, stretching their skin into large flaps that they could use as wings. After that, the birds won all the games. But the bapashkwaanashiinh and the zhagaskaandawe were changed forever—they kept their wings. Today they are known as the bat and the flying squirrel, and they remain the only four-legged animals in our area that fly. The game was now so one-sided in favor of the birds that it was handed over to the Ojibwe, who always remember the lesson of humility and include even the smallest players in every game.

Today, lacrosse is still an active part of Ojibwe culture, but it is not nearly as widely practiced. I played in a lacrosse league as a young man, and one of my sons has claimed it as a major passion. But basketball, football, and hockey probably have more traction with Native kids these days.

Lacrosse was customarily a men's game, but there is a women's lacrosse game, too, often called the "women's stick game" in English. It was just as widely and passionately played as the male version. And, as in the male version of lacrosse, there could be dozens of players on each side and a massive pitch (larger than a modern football field) for playing.

I have a big family, and we have several sets of lacrosse gear, so when it's nice out we go outside and play catch or even stage a game. For social functions like this, we have the boys and girls play together.

The Ojibwe and the Dakota used to stage large competitions at Long Prairie, Minnesota. Maude Kegg and others published some great stories about the wagers and the use of medicine to win in foot races. Now it is more likely that our many impressive athletes will participate in school sports or the Indigenous Games—an Indigenous-only Olympic-style event that includes a lot of traditional Indigenous sports as well as track and field. In Lansing, Michigan, and Minneapolis, Minnesota, there are Native lacrosse leagues with multiple teams.

In addition to sport, we have many games of skill and luck. The best known is the Ojibwe moccasin game. A good friend of mine, Charles Grolla, wrote a book detailing the history and rules of the game called *Makazinataagewin: Ojibwe Style Moccasin Game*. The game does have a complex rule book, so I refer you to that for full details. But the essentials of the game are this: Two teams of three players take turns playing offense and defense. The defending team has four moccasins in front of them. Typically, these are now stylized—four decorated cloth rectangles that symbolize the moccasins used in the original game. They also have four musket balls, one of which is colored differently from the others. Today, a lot of players use marbles instead of musket balls. One of the defending players hides one marble under each of the moccasins. Their teammates sing moccasin game songs to distract and tease their opponents. One of the players on offense uses a stick to lift or slap one of the moccasins to say where the unique marble is or isn't. One of their partners uses marbles in their hand to back up the person using the stick. The marbles he holds have one of a different color to show where he thinks the hidden one was placed by the opposing side. They switch roles, playing offense and defense

Showing off our moccasin game equipment. Isaac (holding football), Elias (center), Caleb (back left), Robert (back right), and Evan (front). *Anton Treuer*

for numerous rounds, which vary based on the scoring success of each previous round. It can take hours to play a game. People used to make dramatic bets—horses, large quantities of wild rice, bandolier bags. Today the wagers aren't quite as impressive, but everyone has to ante up something to play.

Younger people often play a bone and needle game that involves both skill and chance. Bones are strung together on a string that's attached to a large needle. People take turns trying to fling the bones and scoop them onto the needle in one motion.

Another game that my kids and I love to play is called bagese. Originally, Wenabozho played this game against evil spirits, winning in dramatic style to defeat them and keep the people safe. It's a game with eight bone figurines: four round figures, one fish, two knives, and a woman. They can be carved out of animal bone or deer antler. All are white on one side and red on the other. The figurines are placed in a large wooden bowl; there are also one hundred scoring sticks. All players ante up—an item of value, money, or even an IOU for chore service. Each player takes a turn shaking the bowl, scoring points based on which figure lands as the only one showing white (or red). The player then wins the appropriate number of scoring sticks. Anyone who gets skunked pays the ante a second time and sits out that round. The game goes around the circle until someone gets all the sticks and all the loot. There is one play that can end the game early: if someone makes the woman stand straight up in the bowl, it's an automatic victory and usually a ten-minute guffaw, complete with war whoops. Since bagese is a less common game and a really fun part of our culture, I've put the rules in an appendix to this book for those who want to revive the game with their families.

Summer is a short, intense, and formative season in the Ojibwe world. Humans evolve with changes in the weather. We mature and deepen, knowing the best is yet to come.

Elias Treuer. ***Nedahness Greene***

FALL
Adulthood

WHILE SUMMER IS A SEASON of intense growth, nourishment, and tests, fall is an entirely different stage of transition. Some days there is a chill in the air, and the arrival of a cold winter seems imminent. Some days are still blisteringly hot. But with summer fading, fall is also a time of harvest. Joyous but stressful beginnings and sometimes painful tests of maturation come into new light. The trees turn red and gold, and often relationships do, too. In the Ojibwe cycle, this season is characterized by mature love between partners and between parents and their adult children, building careers, and manifesting one's calling in life. The Ojibwe cultural toolbox has much wisdom to share about navigating marriage and divorce, releasing one's children into adulthood, adulting in all its forms, and the trials and triumphs of living in a land of bounty with a harsh and forbidding climate.

Marriage and parenting made me and destroyed me and made me anew. As I write this book, I am entering autumn in my own life. I was too self-absorbed when I was in spring and too busy when I was in summer to really reflect on my life, to step back and look at it from a distance. I now think of what a fool I sometimes was, how I erred and others paid for my mistakes. I think, too, of the times when I showed up as a better version of myself, and how it made all the difference. I grew up as I helped my children grow up, and my son Elias has often been on my mind. He has been a recipient of the kind of blessings and curses that only a father can bestow.

When Elias was born, I was in chaos. I had jumped into my relationship with his mother headfirst after divorcing my first wife, the mother of my daughter Madeline. I never even took the time to assess whether the new relationship was a good fit for me. It wasn't. All my work with Archie Mosay, Tom Stillday, Anna Gibbs, Melvin Eagle, and others was put to the test as I navigated incredible stress. I can see now that she was not a monster, but she had been wounded; she was plagued by monsters and unable to escape the cataclysmic damage of every kind of abuse that can be inflicted on a child. She struggled to show up for me, for herself, and for us in many ways. Shortly after Elias's birth, she descended into the darkness of alcohol and drug abuse, and she never reemerged. In part, it was my mistakes and misjudgment that brought Elias into this world; yet he has been one of the greatest blessings in my life. But there was a price for my mistakes, and it was primarily paid by my son. I brought into this world a child who has no memory of being held or nurtured by his mother.

Elias was just an infant in arms when we retreated to my childhood home—a small cabin, twenty-four feet by twenty-four feet—to restart our life. Elias's three brothers and two sisters came with

The Treuer family cabin. *Robert Treuer*

us. Three of them weren't my biological children, but when their mother fell, I just couldn't leave them to the sometimes cruel winds of fate in the foster care system. The kids slept in a row on the floor of the cabin. It was crowded and cozy and chaotic.

Once we settled in at the cabin, I gathered the kids in the yard and we had a feast. I smoked my pipe and we took turns praying. We prayed for their mom's health and safety. We prayed for the kids. I didn't ask the spirits to keep them with me; I just asked that they be given the best possible chance to have long, healthy, happy lives. We placed an eagle feather on a woven mat next to the food and I asked the spirits to bless the feather and protect our home. They all watched as I put a ladder up on the southwest corner of the cabin and hung that eagle feather on the edge of the eave outside. I told them that my elders said the eagles fly higher than other birds and would watch over and bless our home. The thunderbirds were related to the eagles, and they would know we were living there and pass over our home if there was a tornado or gale-force winds. Elias's siblings seemed a little skeptical, but Elias just stared at me. He hadn't even said his first word yet, but somehow it seemed like he was listening.

It was a humbling time for me. I turned down all offers of consulting work. My kids needed my time and undistracted presence more than my money. We played board games and ate a lot of food. We built forts and played in the woods. I took them to a lot of drum ceremonies. Elias was the youngest, at the bottom of the pecking order. He had both resilience and vulnerability on display. There were springs in the front yard of the cabin, bubbling water into a small stream that flowed into a pond and then on to the Mississippi River. Springs are healing in the Ojibwe world, and that place was healing for all of us.

I had help. My mother and sister lived nearby and helped watch the kids. I kept my job as professor of Ojibwe at Bemidji State

University, and it kept us all fed. The kids and I helped each other, too. We cooked and cleaned and stacked firewood together.

Elias learned how to walk there. When his brother Isaac was potty training, he walked all over the yard and pooped in several places, and Elias walked right behind him and stomped on all the piles of poop. We laughed a lot in those days, too.

Elias always watched me closely when it was ceremony time. He would run around the outside of the house and check the eagle feather hanging off the eave whenever it thundered. The feather on the eave of the house and the dreamcatcher by his bedroll on the floor gave him a measure of steady reassurance. He liked to put tobacco in the water.

Money was often tight, but I took the kids to Bonanza for the all-you-can-eat buffet once in a while. I usually asked to be put in the back, far away from other humans. But at least one of the kids usually had to go all the way to the front of the restaurant to use the washroom. Isaac once ran back through the restaurant and up to each table, yelling at top volume, repeatedly, "I took a crap! I took a crap!" While I was distracted with Isaac, Elias carefully smuggled mac and cheese from the buffet in the pockets of his pants. Another time, I couldn't get Elias's hands through his coat sleeves when it was time to go because his hands were bunched in fists. I had to ask, "Baby, what's in your hands?"

"I got the mac and cheese," came his husky-voiced reply, and then he shoveled the mac into his mouth before I could take it away.

As entertaining as the antics were, they spoke to an underlying pain for all the kids. Their mom was alive, but they had lost her all the same. And if they could lose someone that important, they could lose anything. Hoarding extra mac and cheese wasn't just kids being "deep rez," it was also a strategy for security, an insurance plan in case there wasn't enough later or something or someone was taken away.

Anna Gibbs liked to come check up on her namesakes, and Elias was one of her favorites. She enjoyed watching the kids play warrior games and made them get her snacks and drinks and extra blankets. It was obvious to everyone how overwhelmed I was. But I think she could sense that underneath the laughter and high energy coming from the kids was a kind of hunger, an unmet need.

She told me there was a ceremony for making families strong. She said that I wasn't just a young man anymore. I had to master this ceremony. It would settle the kids and make everything right. She had my attention.

Anna was notoriously obsessed with details when it came to ceremony, and her instructions for doing a bear smoke were no exception. I gathered the white rocks, tiny cups, red willow tobacco, and willow sticks. I had the kids help me make a miniature wigwam on the top of a large hill behind the cabin. We put tobacco on the floor of the mini wigwam and then made little rafts of willow sticks for each of us, similar to those we customarily made for water ceremonies. We each put an item of our used clothes on top. We lined the rocks in front, symbolizing stepping-stones for various stages of life. We made food offerings and I smoked my pipe. The bear is the chief of the land animals; it is a sacred animal. There are stories about bears being humans transformed into animal form and humans who are bears transformed into Anishinaabeg. The body of a skinned bear looks eerily human. We invoked the bears to watch over our family and to unite us in one wigwam, to accept our offerings in that miniature lodge as evidence of our cohesion and security. We sat around on the bare ground and ate the food. The kids started to wrestle and run through the tall pines on top of the hill. Elias kept returning to look at the little wigwam and smile.

Things went better after that. I got a construction loan, and we jacked up the cabin and moved it to another land parcel, replacing it with a new house. The kids grew and grew. My career took off.

I fell in love with Blair and remarried. More children joined our big, blended horde. There were nine kids total by the time we were done. Elias was thriving. He was one of the best students in his class all the way through grade, middle, and high school. He developed a beautiful baritone voice and joined show choir, winning numerous singing competitions for team and solo performances of every kind. He was an avid hunter, too, as adept in the woods as he was on the stage.

When the COVID-19 pandemic hit, Elias had some big tests. He was finishing his junior year of high school, and his rich social experience was turned upside down. All musical performances at the school were canceled. He went through a painful breakup with his girlfriend. And now he had nowhere to go and lots of time to think about all of that and everything else that had happened in his life.

As a parent, I know that all kids have to break from their parents, to become independent. I tried to shift from being the supervisor of their lives to being a coach, and then only if they wanted me to do it. The girls seemed to go through their maturation break a little younger than the boys. Their bodies changed earlier, and the hormonal and emotional transformations converged then. The boys seemed to break a little later, often right when it was time to develop launch plans and apply to colleges.

I was worried about Elias. It was more than a worry about getting into college or making a successful launch. I worried that maybe the feather on the corner of the house, and the bear smoke, and the rest of the cultural toolbox wasn't enough. I worried that what had happened with his mother would haunt him or pull him away from the light. Maybe he wouldn't feel safe leaving or would deny himself opportunity in favor of familiarity. Elias was pensive and withdrawn for a time. But I pushed him for a plan, and he stepped up and took charge. The cultural toolbox had delivered the goods after all. He wanted to apply to Dartmouth College, early admission. While the other Ivy League schools had a lot to offer, he loved the idea of a community of Native undergraduates with some shared experiences, struggles, and dreams, and the other Ivies didn't have that as much as Dartmouth. He brooded and bent over his computer for weeks and then produced one of the most stunning things I've ever read.

Rather than ignoring the painful chapters of his history, he leaned in to his personal journey and wrote a powerful, gut-wrenching essay about his loss—the times it hurt and the times he didn't feel anything at all. He contextualized his experience. He spoke of the experience his ancestors had with genocide, the experience his relatives had in residential boarding schools and (on my father's side) the Holocaust. He articulated a dream for his future and said that the cycle of trauma would stop with him. I believed him. This was his truth and his destiny, and he has made it visibly manifest every day since.

The kids were all at the kitchen island when I got home a few weeks later, and Elias said that his decision letter had arrived. He hadn't opened it yet. Our twelve-year-old, Mia, started recording on a smartphone. Elias hesitated, paced back and forth, and then started reading the first words before he shouted, "Let's go!" He folded me into a tight embrace; I was crying. People tell me that I somehow saved my kids from the darkness—rebuilding my family, creating a new marriage, showing them our ways. But it was always the other way around. Every time Elias ran around the house to check on our eagle feather when he was three, he wasn't just reassuring himself—he was reinvigorating my confidence in the cultural toolbox. Every time he stopped to stare at the little wigwam from our bear smoke and smile, he was building my faith. It was he who showed us what it looked like to come out of fear and scarcity into abundance, out of the darkness and into the light. I didn't save him; he saved me. So, I cried tears of heartfelt joy, cathartic relief, and unbridled pride. We posted the video to social media, and the rest of the world must have needed some good news in the middle of the pandemic, too. It was viewed over one hundred thousand times and sent a flood of messages to my ecstatic son and his very proud father. Fall has always been my favorite season.

MARRIAGE AND RELATIONSHIPS

In precontact Ojibwe communities, romantic relationships, dating, courtship, and marriage had far fewer rules and less social pressure than in most parts of Europe and Asia. That doesn't mean everyone was in a freer state then; life could be hard, and being married made it easier for adults to maintain resources. There were significantly fewer men than women in those days because of warfare and dangerous travel. Both men and women fought and traveled, but war was a male-dominated pursuit, and men usually transported the winter fur harvests long distances to bring them to trade posts, risking enemy attacks, accidents, and dangerous weather conditions far from home. As a result, polygamy was an accepted custom and not uncommon.

I'm more interested in showing you how the Ojibwe cultural toolbox can be applied to a modern life than a detailed analysis of its history, but it's worth noting that relationships and marriage in Ojibwe culture have changed a lot over time. When French fur traders came to Ojibwe country in the middle of the 1600s, the Ojibwe encouraged them—and the French fur trade bosses often required them—to marry Ojibwe women to cement economic and political alliances. A lot of babies were made that way. Even today, about one-third of Ojibwe people have French surnames. The Ojibwe never even carried surnames until the French arrived. Now most have first, middle, and last names, and Ojibwe names. We are multicultural at many levels from that experience.

The Ojibwe had patriarchy issues before the French arrived, but European contact changed marriage dynamics, and patriarchy grew. Ojibwe women had a lot of say in who they would marry before this and had full freedom to divorce their husbands. Ceremonial lodges (sweat lodge, medicine dance lodge, ceremonial drum dance hall) were considered communal property and owned by everyone in the village, but family dwellings were different. The Ojibwe were matrilocal—the woman owned the wigwam. All she had to do was set her husband's stuff outside the door and that was a divorce. It didn't happen that often, but it happened. Women who were married to French traders came under pressure to accommodate. Their children were often raised Catholic, especially the boys, who were put to work in the French fur trade as traders and translators when they grew up. And the French husbands then sought to control the marriage fates of their daughters. Many more Ojibwe people were now born into the eagle and marten clans, the adopting clans for people with non-Native fathers. Many more Ojibwe men were excluded from consideration for tribal leadership by the circumstances of their births.

The cultural impact of French-Ojibwe marriage and military, political, and economic intermingling was profound. It gave birth to the Métis, a new cultural group that was culturally and biologically hybrid—French and Ojibwe, but including people and cultural influences from other tribes and European settlers, too. Other offspring from these French and Ojibwe unions were absorbed into either French or Ojibwe communities, but both mother cultures were transformed through their influence.

Men's gender roles, such as warfare, continued to put them at more risk. As a result, polygamy remained an Ojibwe custom throughout the 1800s. The custom was supported by the practical realities of there being more women than men and also the cultural norms that grew in response to that reality. A higher burden was placed on women to orchestrate the provisioning that was customarily a male enterprise or an enterprise they shared with men. These dynamics both stressed and strengthened aspects of Ojibwe culture. But eventually, gender numbers began to balance, missionaries and Indian agents began to force changes, and Ojibwe marriage customs more and more resembled those of the French, British, and American colonists around them.

Even while the arc of Ojibwe cultural practices in love and marriage has trended toward alignment with European customs, many teachings and practices in the Ojibwe cultural toolbox around relationships and marriage are still practiced and have relevance for an Anishinaabe person trying to live a cultural life today.

The metaphor of four seasons we apply to a person's life also has application to the lives of relationships. Spring in a romantic relationship is when everything is new—verdant growth, soulful exploration, and an explosion of energy and connection. It's an exciting, intoxicating time. Summer can burn long and hot. This is when couples are making and raising babies, worrying about money and houses. The excitement of new love gives way to sustained communication, mutual reliance, friendship, and teamwork. It's less sexy and more sustaining. It's also a time of tests in relationships. The glue between a couple is deeper, but less intense. The stress of child-raising and work and money often exposes cracks in communication and shared values. Fall is a season of maturing love. For couples who make it here, there is a harvest. Some of the stresses fade. A deeper connection and friendship and history hold the couple together. Winter in relationships is characterized by true wisdom, long shared history, children having children, and legacy.

Relationships can thrive or fail at any season in the union for many different reasons, but some people struggle because they think relationships are only about spring. They bounce from one partner to another looking for the intensity and intoxication of new love. Some relationships buckle under the stresses of dealing with money and child-raising. People drift apart—or drift into someone else's embrace. But for those who understand the beauty and challenges of each season in a relationship, the toolbox can help make a marriage thrive. I haven't had a relationship with my wife, Blair—I have had many relationships with her, through the seasons of one marriage.

Archie told me that in the late 1800s, when his father was courting his mother, he used to walk from East Lake, near McGregor, Minnesota, to Balsam Lake, Wisconsin, to visit. The walk took him three days each way. When he got to Balsam Lake, the couple went for walks, but his future wife's aunts walked a few paces behind them to make sure they weren't misbehaving. He kept that up for a couple years before everyone in their families approved of the union. Then he moved to Wisconsin and they started a family.

People these days are not nearly so patient and give much less power to their families in approving of a marriage. But it is wise to take time during the honeymoon phases of a relationship to consider whether you have shared values with your partner. Building a strong friendship, not just a strong attraction, is also important.

Archie taught that the first seven marriages created the first seven clans. The taboo against marrying someone of the same clan is still a big one in Ojibwe culture today, although I have run into a couple of notable exceptions. You probably won't lose your job or be shunned socially, but you will likely be the subject of reproach and gossip at some level. Instead of leading with, "Hey baby, what's your sign?" it's always better to ask, "Hey baby, what's your clan?" Even within the twenty clans we have now, opposites are thought to make good spiritual chemistry. Someone from one of the bird clans is a good match for one of the fish or animal clans—bear and eagle, wolf and bullhead, and so forth.

The Ojibwe flute and hand drum were often used in courtship. Like birds preening feathers, Ojibwe men tried to draw attention from a potential lover and communicate through song. This wasn't a requirement in traditional courtship, but it was an extra dose of magic for those who could play.

In Ojibwe, the partner words are pretty practical in meaning. *Wiijiwaagan* means "partner," and we use that word for romantic partners of any gender and sometimes for partners in nonromantic settings. On ceremonial drums, often more than one person is seated in a certain position or duty on the drum, and they call one another wiijiwaagan. *Wiidigemaagan* literally means "housemate," and it's one of the most common words for "spouse." This really can be used for your college roommate, too, even though it's usually heard with reference to married partners. *Ninaabem* means "my man." *Indikwem* means "my woman." *Niwiiw* is "my wife," and there is no male counterpart to that word other than *ninaabem*. *Niinimoshenh* means "my cousin of the opposite sex" and sometimes is also used for "my sweetheart." That dual usage sometimes makes people laugh and wonder about its origin, but nonromantic friends of the opposite gender were usually referred to by a term of relation, and the usage probably shifted as a result of attempted discretion when people were courting.

In former times there wasn't much to Ojibwe wedding ceremonies. People just moved in together; being someone's housemate meant being their spouse. No paperwork. No name changes. No officiating required.

Archie said that while marriage ceremonies are not needed, there is nothing wrong with blessing a couple when they get married. He ended up officiating at quite a few weddings over the years. He used a blanket to symbolize the couple's shared home and wrapped them in it to unite them. He smoked his pipe, mentioned their different clans, and asked the spirits to bless them.

Blair and I smoke a two-stemmed pipe together as Dennis Jones officiates at our wedding. ***Dustin Burnette***

My elders remembered people getting married at the ceremonial drums in the first half of the 1900s as well, with the use of special songs and the couple dancing around the drum together to show the community that they were married. This practice seems to have dropped off over the past several decades. I go to drum ceremonies all the time, and I have never seen a wedding done there.

When Blair and I got married, we had our ceremony done much as Archie would have done it—with a blanket and pipe ceremony. But my wife had a classic wedding dress, and I had a tuxedo as well. Our officiant, Dennis Jones, had a special pipe for the ceremony with two stems, so we could smoke it together at the same time.

I get asked to officiate at weddings, too, now, and it's always an honor. I follow Archie's protocol with the blanket and blessing and usually explain to the couple about the seasons in a relationship. Sometimes the couple wants music, and we bring in a powwow drum or sing on hand drums.

BEING AN OJIBWE WOMAN

Gender identity can be complex and nuanced—there are more than two ways that people identify themselves. But historic Ojibwe communities separated gender identity from the division of labor and spiritual responsibilities. People didn't care if someone was gay or lesbian or transgender or any of the many varied gender identities that existed then and now. But they had to pick from two primary sets of duties. Male responsibilities included war, long-distance travel, and big game hunting. Female responsibilities focused on food storage, clothing manufacture, and the raising of small children. Building wigwams and many staple harvests, such as maple and wild rice, involved everyone in the community of all ages and genders. This was a pattern, rather than a rule book. There are many stories and historical references to people who were not cisgender but still lived lives in one of these primary gender roles.

Today, the Ojibwe world, like many cultures, has started to accommodate these nuances better. But in terms of spiritual roles, the division remains.

I remember reading the work of Catharine MacKinnon in college and being impressed by her analysis of how American and European cultures kept men and women separated as a means of keeping women in inferior power positions throughout history. I went with my mother to a ceremony at Brokenhead First Nation in Manitoba and met up with my namesake Mary Roberts there. At the ceremony they separated us: men were to sit on one side of the ceremony lodge and women on the other. I knew what MacKinnon would say about that. But I was curious what my namesake had to say, so I asked. Her answer was simple: "We sit on different sides of the lodge to remind ourselves that women and men each own half this lodge."

Over the years I have thought of Mary's response often. In Ojibwe culture, empowerment of both women and men happens not through equality, but through balance. There is actually a weakness to the argument that women can and should do anything a man can. The weakness is that this argument sets up what men do (patriarchy) as the ultimate goal for women. And often women pressure themselves to reinforce patriarchy instead of affirming their empowerment in their own right. This happens on the racial landscape, too, as people of color try to look and act "white" to access power and prestige and profits, rather than affirming their own racial identity and its empowerment. It's more empowering to have women redefine their sources of empowerment on their own terms, rather than in response to patriarchy. I think the Ojibwe cultural toolbox does a remarkable job at that.

Water is a central element in female power. The moon is often referred to as grandmother, and she moves the water here on earth.

It is the moon that makes tides in the ocean. In Lake Superior, the moon creates a smaller (five-centimeter) tide twice each day and contributes to the seiche on the big lake, an irregular oscillating wave. The moon pulls at all water on the planet, even though it is only the big bodies of water that show a discernable tide. A glass of water on the table is being pulled by the moon. The water in everyone's body is being pulled by the moon, too.

When women live together, their menstrual periods often gravitate to the same cycle, and each woman has her own spiritual gravity that shapes the flow of water. On a raw kinetic and spiritual level their bodies start to flow together, and together they are pulled by the moon in a similar rhythm.

The Ojibwe have many types of drum ceremonies, and one is called ikwe-dewe'igan, meaning "woman drum." This ceremony is associated with grandmother moon. It has multiple purposes, but one is to restore balance between women and men. The drum chiefs in this ceremony are women (a male role on other ceremonial drums). There is a special kind of dancing that everyone engages in at these ceremonies, usually called ikwe-niimiwin, "the woman dance." Both men and women dance to these songs as a means of restoring balance, but women always start the dances and initiate everyone into the circle by the giving of gifts. The ikwe-dewe'igan is the only drum ceremony whose woman songs can be sung during either the day or the night—on all other drums, the songs are for nighttime use only. From the ikwe-dewe'igan, the woman dance spread to all the other ceremonial drums in our area. There, too, it is female drum members who start the dance. It's done at night because that's when the moon is up, visible, and strongest. She pulls at the water in every woman's body to get her up and dancing, swaying in common rhythm, and sends all of the people into motion. This is the spiritual current of the dances. When you visit, you will see exchanges of gifts, circles of dancers around the drum, bobbing up and down to the syncopated beat of the songs and laughing.

In the pregnancy and childbirth section I mentioned how babies are carried in water and born out of water from the womb. It's a natural assumption that water is women's domain. At some kinds of ceremonies, a special blessing of water is customarily done by women.

The mantra "water is life" is an ancient understanding for many Indigenous peoples. It's a fact, of course. The water leaves our bodies when we die. And protecting it is not just practical (we all need water to drink and grow food); it is spiritual.

When the moon is full, grandmother is pulling at us all with great force. A lot of people have trouble sleeping for a few days at the peak of the lunar cycle. In our circle, there is a special ceremony that the women have, usually called a full moon ceremony. I've been to these at a distance many times. My mother made me build and keep fire for her full moon ceremonies for years. Women of all ages gather around a fire at night. They have a prayer circle. My mom used to keep everyone's hair throughout the month—whatever came out when brushing or trimming—and at the moon ceremony she tied it in a yellow cloth and fed it to the fire. It always felt very powerful to see my mother, sister, daughters, and granddaughter gather together for these ceremonies. It's not uncommon to have three, four, or five generations in a family do these together.

There are special challenges to being a woman. From outside female space come demeaning acts of sexual objectification and the risk of sexual predation. From inside female space comes competition from other women, who sometimes lose focus on the flow of positive energy between women and shame, ridicule, or ostracize one another. There is pressure on women to compete with men for equal political and economic power, and there are attacks (from both men and women) if they succeed. Whatever path a woman chooses in her life—to marry or not, have children or not, have any kind of career or not, engage in socially defined feminine or masculine pursuits—the Ojibwe cultural toolbox offers opportunity to women for deep spiritual grounding and community to traverse all terrains.

BEING AN OJIBWE MAN

While water is a central element in the spiritual power of women, fire is the spiritual domain of men. The sun is considered a male energy. All growing things need both male and female energies. Plants need water and sunlight. Procreation requires contributions from both male and female. Men are especially encouraged to wake with the sun. It burns off confusion and grief and provides spiritual strength.

As boys transition into manhood, they are often given a flint and steel and taught about caretaking spirit fire. It is customarily a male duty to build and watch sacred fires at sweat lodges, wakes, and funerals, and even at female ceremonies such as the full moon ceremony. A sacred fire is a portal to the spirit world, and we only want to send good things there. So, male firekeepers usually honor a certain protocol about the fire. Tobacco and feast food can be burned—it's like giving your grandfather a smoke or a meal. But garbage, cigarette butts, and newspaper do not belong in sacred fire. Those fires are started with flint and steel, by rubbing sticks (which can create a fire in less than ten seconds when done right), or with matches. And they are fed by birchbark and wood. When putting tobacco in a fire, people sometimes burn cedar or other medicine with it to purify the good thoughts being sent through the fire portal.

Men carry a spiritual spark, an internal fire, as well. We are told to initiate action. Often this can be as simple as starting a game with the kids, throwing the first snowball in a snowball fight, asking someone on a date, or lighting a ceremonial pipe. Some of the strongest bonding moments with all my kids have come through times of action—sitting next to each of them for their first deer kills, taking a trip, even just doing chores.

Both men and women have decisions to make, courses to chart in their lives. But women are born with their water power, which naturally flows and grows as they age. Men are born with a spark, but fires don't grow naturally without fuel. Untended fires go out, so men have a burden that is different from that of women. They have to take their natural spark, kindle a fire, and keep adding fuel to it throughout their lives. This is why men are usually pressured to fast—to see what kind of fire they should build. Both men and women can fast. Both can find purpose and drive in doing so. But men have to rely on it to find purpose even more than women.

The messages men receive about what it means to be a man are sometimes misleading and confusing. We are often told to be strong, to be good providers, to protect everyone, to be warriors. But we hear the opposite, too—to be nonviolent, to be vulnerable, to be kind and accommodating. There is a cultural pushing match over the very definition of manhood. And there are pushes coming from multiple directions, even within our cultural communities.

When the ceremonial big drum came to the Ojibwe, it was a gift from the Dakota—a peace offering. Initially all of the Ojibwe men who were seated as singers, chiefs, warriors, speakers, and messengers (all formal positions on the drums) were Ojibwe men who had killed Dakota. They were told that someday the Ojibwe would run out of people who had that experience, and that was good. When that happened, they should seat Ojibwe men who had served in the armed forces or been in other kinds of combat, but someday they would run out of people who had that experience, too, and that was good. The drums are a pathway to peace. The primary purpose of warriors was to lead the people to peace. And peace would never be obtainable until the warriors led that charge.

Today veterans are often sought after to assume duties on our ceremonial drums. Even at powwows and many other functions, veterans are asked to lead. We have them carry flags and eagle staffs, lead the grand entry at powwows, perform special duties at funerals, and be available to advise and counsel people who are grieving. Outsiders see how special veterans are in Ojibwe communities, and they sometimes misunderstand that as glorifying combat, but it's actually the opposite. For all men—veterans or not—the toolbox encourages us to embrace peace and tells warriors to lead us there.

Embracing peace was not always the Ojibwe way. We fought bloody wars with the Haudenosaunee and Dakota. Violence was not just a manifestation of colonization—it was something we did for a long time. The Ojibwe scalped before whites came to our shores. The archaeological record makes that clear, as do the attestations of the earliest recorded contacts with Europeans. But colonization amplified the violence, no doubt. The scale of conflict and the technologies we used to wage war got more deadly after Europeans arrived. We were complex people. We were not more warlike than other people or other races, but we were likely not less warlike, either. The introduction of the medicine dance and the ceremonial drums provided an intentional Indigenous redefinition of what it meant to be a man and what it meant to be a warrior. There may be some who provide different messaging on this topic, but it is clear to me: the Ojibwe cultural toolbox teaches that the way of the warrior is peace. I accept the redefining effort of my ancestors who embraced the lodge and the drums. It's my way now, too. I'm an imperfect participant in our teachings, but I do try to align my life with this code.

The way of a soldier is one of conformity: following orders, wearing a uniform, having the same haircut as one's brothers in arms. But the way of the warrior is about individuality. Ojibwe warriors often had unique medicines, paint, and sacred items for protection and guidance. As we move toward peace, we never lose our need for warriors; the duties of warriors shift, but not the importance of warriors themselves. I keep a warrior bundle now with items that I've dreamed about. Many other Ojibwe men learn about and earn the right to carry the claws of the crow, hawk, coyote, wolf, and bear. Some use war paint and others do not. But the teachings accumulated through other seasons in a man's life are still centered in fall—the importance of caretaking, protection, instruction, and provisioning are not just male ethos. They are responsibilities that Ojibwe men are encouraged to center in their lives.

There are special challenges for Ojibwe men. Men of color are subjected to a special kind of fear. I'm a friendly guy, but it's common for me to see that someone is locking the car door in the parking lot when I walk by. Men of color are far less safe when dealing with police than are people of any other group. It is sometimes hard for men to find any circle where they can be affirmed and supported without question. Women can be mean to one another at times, but they are far more likely to compliment one another on their appearance or upon happy news. Men are more likely to tease one another or even be adversarial. It leaves a lot of men feeling rather alone. I try to maintain this awareness when I banter with my buddies, so that I can be a positive force in their lives. We have to be intentional about how we carry ourselves with one another. The toolbox helps here, too. When Ojibwe men gather for lacrosse or moccasin game competitions, we can build our fires and engage our competitive dispositions without harming one another. We can use sweat lodges and men's gatherings to affirm one another, share teachings, and support our individual and group growth. I have a circle of adult men who gather to do exactly that. We all rely on that space to learn and to spark one another's follow-through on bear smoke ceremonies, water ceremonies, and other regular offerings. The cultural toolbox provides support, guidance, and initiative to men. It helps us be the best versions of ourselves.

PARENTING

I think about parenting all the time since it's been such a defining part of my life, and I've spread teachings about parenting throughout this book. As my children have aged, I have realized more and more that the receiving is in the giving. I have been healed over and over by healing others. My inner child has healed by helping my own children. I encourage all parents to pick up teachings and tools in the spring and summer sections and apply them to their own journey through the seasons.

In the Ojibwe world we are often told to look at how the four-legged animals and birds parent. The porcupines are the most notoriously bad parents in the animal kingdom; they leave their babies for days on end to climb trees and eat bark. If someone sees a fellow human being neglectful, calling them a porcupine would be a major insult. But we mainly have positive examples of parenting in nature. Most birds mate for life and make attentive parents. Bears are protective of their young. Wolves show us the importance of extended family and communal living.

HAIR

Hair is special in the Ojibwe world. It is private and intimate. In former times people took care not to leave their hair lying around. It's leaving your spiritual energy scattered all over the place for people to disregard—poor spiritual hygiene. If someone was married, it was taboo to have someone other than family handle their hair. Today, a lot of Ojibwe people see barbers and beauticians for haircuts, perms, lashes, and waxing like the rest of the world. But other than that, most people still just have family touch their hair.

My mother gathered everyone's hair from combs and haircuts and kept it in a little can in the bathroom. When it was time for full moon ceremonies, she tied it in yellow cloth and burned it. Nancy Jones, another respected mentor of mine, balls hers up and puts it in the branch of a tree. Others bury it.

Leonard Moose, an esteemed elder from Mille Lacs, said that hair is each person's private medicine. When he was a kid, if someone had a haircut, they would run the end of the cut braid across a hot rock to cauterize the "wound" so their medicine wouldn't leak out.

Today hair is also part of identity. There are a lot of brown people in our part of the world, but long hair, especially on men, commonly indicates Native as opposed to Latinx, Arab, or Asian ethnicity, especially when worn with some beads or braids.

In former times, the Ojibwe did not show excessive vanity when they had a death in the family. For the caretaking of hair, that often meant not braiding for an extended period of time. People washed up—they were hygienic. But sometimes there was a wicked tangle, and some people cut their hair. In Round Lake, Wisconsin, this became ritualized—a small piece of hair was cut at night, at the ceremonial drum, and then kept with the person's bundle for a year. For some of the Plains tribes, a haircut is a required part of the mourning ritual. That's less the case with the Ojibwe, but the association is well known here. Because of all these traditions involving hair and death, it is taboo to get a haircut at night, unless it's with the intent of engaging in a mourning ritual. To do so when not in mourning is like telling the spirits, "I want to be in mourning."

BEAR SMOKE

The bear smoke ceremony that I did with Elias and his siblings is something that Ojibwe people used to do annually. Customarily it is done in the spring, after the frost goes out and the bears are done sleeping and on the move. It's good to pick a clean place that's in the woods, rather than in the yard. It's considered more inviting to the spirits of the bears. This ceremony is to seek the protection of the bear, but also to strengthen families and provide for their safety and unity. More than one family can do this ceremony at the same time, but if there is more than one family, each family builds its own miniature wigwam. Now that some of my children are becoming parents, they build their own wigwams for bear smoke, and we set them up next to one another.

The wigwams are small, just a foot high and a foot wide and a couple feet long. We usually use hazel brush and tie the sticks with basswood bark or ripped cloth ties. We offer tobacco to each piece of hazel brush we harvest. Hazel brush is simply prolific where we live; if maple, ironwood, or willow is more readily available, they work, too. The door, placed on one of the short ends of the wigwam, faces east. We create a bed of shaved willow bark inside the wigwam. We use diamond or red willow, which are cousins and accepted as offerings. We use the shaved sticks, about the diameter of a pinky finger, and cut them down to four-inch lengths. Using yarn, we tie ten of the four-inch sticks together to make a miniature raft for each family member. Then we place an item of used clothing on each raft and place the rafts inside the wigwam.

In front of the east door of the wigwam, we place ten small stones. These are stepping-stones, representing cultural milestones in a person's life. They are usually light in color (white or light gray), flat, and no bigger than a half dollar in diameter. They are lined up from south to north immediately in front of the east door of the wigwam. We use either maple sap or maple syrup with water added to form reconstituted sap and place a small Dixie cup of the liquid for each family member in front of the door.

We cook food and often try to find things a bear would like—a bowl of fresh blueberries, a meat dish, fish. Then we pass tobacco to the family members. If anyone is a pipe carrier, they bring their own pipe. Then someone prays, invoking the spirits and making special mention of the bear as chief of the land animals to watch over the family and keep the family strong. We usually sit around on the ground. If a family has a place where they do this ceremony every year, they sometimes place a stone in each of the cardinal directions and leave them there to mark their bear smoke spot. The wigwams and stepping-stones and maple offerings and cups are left there for the bears. Each year we make a new offering in the same place, but the remnants of the past year's offering are left undisturbed.

PROTECTION

People can treat us well or treat us poorly. The best protection is to be good to people. If someone is toxic, try to avoid them. But nobody should have to avoid their ceremonies just to stay away from a toxic person. When you have to be around toxic people, or when in unfamiliar company, a few simple precautions can help.

In the Ojibwe way, personal things can render you vulnerable when someone has access and bad intentions. So, people are cautioned to throw their garbage away—dispose of your kids' diapers and your other personal refuse. Shake hands. It's an act of kindness and disarms people in a good way. Be considerate. For an extra measure, some people use various kinds of protection medicine. Many people put a sprig of cedar in their moccasins or shoes. Other people have special medicines in a pouch, in their pocket, hanging from their neck, or sewn into a small piece of fabric in a thimble with a hole drilled in the top and string running from the medicine, through the thimble, and then safety-pinned to their clothes. These are usually blessed in a ceremony and given under direction of a spiritual leader, so I won't list off all of the options. It's better to approach them spiritually with a tobacco offering, rather than scientifically from a list.

There are spirits everywhere, and that's a good thing. Just because something goes bump in the night doesn't mean it's bad luck, bad medicine, or a problem. There is no such thing as a bad dream. Even the dreams that scare us are good. When we dream of the death of a relative, it's often the spirits giving them a little shot of life. When a dream causes real fear, share it with someone. That dilutes its power and helps release the fear. People who have a persistent bad dream sometimes put out a bowl of food and pray over it with tobacco for help, understanding, and protection. If someone dreams about relatives who have passed on, it is customary to make a food offering, to feed the dead—more on that in the winter section.

In extreme cases of distress, fear, or insecurity, people might invite a spiritual leader to their house for a full-fledged pipe ceremony, which includes a smudging of the person who is having a hard time and of their home. Sometimes this involves a house blessing as well.

KEEPING HOUSE

There are a lot of teachings about the blessing, protection, and spiritual maintenance of a home. These vary quite a bit, but the core concepts are pretty universal across Ojibwe country. When someone establishes a new home, moves, or experiences a new chapter in life (new housemates, romantic partner, or kids), it's common to bless one's home.

We usually bless our homes with a pipe ceremony. I bless an eagle feather and put it on the southwest corner of the home as a beacon to let the thunderbirds know to protect the dwelling and its people. A lot of people hang a sprig of cedar over each door and window to filter spiritual visitors and let only the good ones in. We often hang dreamcatchers by the beds of small children to let the good dreams come through and catch the bad ones in a web. Some families build a small wigwam or tipi in the backyard so the spirits will know it's a Native home and watch over it. The spirits do love Anishinaabeg. A lot of families also cut a long cedar pole, often twelve feet in length, dig a hole, place tobacco in it, and then erect the pole in the yard. It's a protection measure, but it also doubles as a place to offer tobacco for daily prayer. I have one with a ribbon for each of my kids, my wife, and myself. It's also customary to have an image of the animals, birds, or fish that represent the clans of the house placed somewhere prominent. Our clans watch over us, and acknowledging them helps keep us in their good graces.

As a matter of routine spiritual maintenance, we smudge with sage from time to time. We use other medicines during hard times, when we are grieving, or when someone has a dream that warrants a higher level of intervention. Some families mark the circle around their yard with ribbons in each of the cardinal directions and a ring of tobacco with an opening where people approach if there seems to be a stretch of bad luck. When COVID-19 came to our area, we placed tobacco ties over the doorways tied in cloth and asked for protection from the disease.

Keeping house requires some basic upkeep. Good spirits are attracted to cleanliness. Bad spirits hide under clutter and are attracted to strong smells. In addition to the details, it's important to mind your disposition. Home is a sacred place. Make it a place you love. Take care of it. Create a warm, inviting space, and good luck, good spirits, and good people will want to be there.

FALL HARVEST

I shared in previous sections how food is medicine. The precontact Ojibwe diet was rich, varied, and extremely healthy. Many people enjoyed longevity in former times that is rare to see in our communities today, and that was before any vaccinations and without hospitals. We were physically active and ate healthy food. With the advancements in modern medicine and vaccinations, we should live even longer. But we have to do our part and make healthy choices. By the time we enter the fall season of our lives, eating habits, exercise habits, and other lifestyle choices start to show their positive or negative effects. The cultural toolbox can help keep us grounded and geared for longevity.

Fall is the most abundant harvest time in the Ojibwe calendar. Wild rice is an obvious example. In some areas, it ripens as early as late August; in most places, it's ready in September. Loaded with nutrients, fiber, and protein, this is a superfood, and it's Ojibwe soul food. Prophets told us to move to the land where food grows on water.

Every kind of hunting is prime in the fall. Small game animals are fat and numerous. Ducks and geese start to migrate and gather in large numbers. Deer, elk, moose, and bear are plump and easiest to hunt during their fall movement patterns. Fish are on the move, too, and the Ojibwe of the past relied on fish even more than hunting. Crops of corn, beans, and squash are ready to harvest.

Methods of harvest have changed over time, as have the technologies available to us. In former times, people spent thousands of hours harvesting nettles, fashioning them into thin string, and then weaving fishnets. Today, most people buy monofilament fishing line and weave nets in a fraction of the time or buy prefabricated nets that are commercially made in a factory. It makes for efficient harvest. People used fish traps as well. That's less common now, although netting is still widely practiced.

I like to hunt with a bow. The season starts earlier, and I can hunt without freezing. But it takes a lot of patience and time. I hunt with a bow in September and October and with a rifle when the season opens in November. My kids prefer rifle hunting, although Evan likes to go out with a bow, too. (The only reason Ojibwe people didn't use rifles before European contact is that they didn't have them yet.) In Red Lake, tribal members can legally hunt deer at night. The deer are active then, and shining a light on them causes them to pause for a second. Good hunters make efficient and reliable kills that way. In many other parts of Ojibwe country, hunting at night is frowned upon. Nighttime is daytime for the spirits of the dead, and shooting something at night might risk shooting at a spirit deer. That's certainly not a universal concern, but it is a concern for some Ojibwe hunters. Personally, I don't hunt at night, but I have no judgments of those who do. Remember that in Ojibwe country, while hunting is fun, we aren't hunting for sport. We are hunting for food.

The Ojibwe have always shaped their environment. We used fire to extend the range of the bison into the woodlands and to burn off underbrush so blueberries could spread. We seeded medicines near villages and transplanted trees. Our ability to do this more efficiently has improved with new technologies. Today the Red Lake Ojibwe maintain a commercial walleye fishery and actively restock fish in the lake for a sustainable harvest. We thin and maintain tree plantations and sugarbush acreage to increase yield in traditional harvests. We manage forests for wildlife sustainability, not just for logging profits. Band members at Leech Lake, Bois Forte, White Earth, and Fond du Lac Reservations all harvest wild rice by the tens of thousands of pounds every year. There are commercial sale operations and reseeding programs. We have the potential to apply the toolbox on a grander scale. But there are barriers. Eighty-five percent of the Leech Lake Reservation is inside the Chippewa

Evan and Isaac with their fall harvest. *Anton Treuer*

Isaac parches rice in our yard. ***Blair Treuer***

National Forest, and its resources are managed by the federal government rather than the tribe. The government just cuts the trees and keeps the money. But all of the tribes have natural resource management agencies and plans, and our environmental ethics can influence how things are managed.

I am as busy as I've ever been. It would be easiest for me to just buy all my food at the store, and we do buy some food at the store and eat at restaurants, but we try to get as much from the woods and water as we reasonably can. I take the kids out to harvest wild rice. We parch it in a giant cast iron kettle in the yard. I often buy extra green rice from my cousins, and if I'm short on time to process it myself, I get it processed at a mill. Our teenage hunters are all successful every fall. We go after ducks and grouse. We fish. We forage for mushrooms. We pick berries. It's a lifestyle choice and it takes time. But being active and in the woods keeps us healthy and more recognizable to our ancestors. And eating that food makes us a little less reliant on the chemically treated, bioengineered stuff sold in stores. The companies that sell seeds and fertilizers to farmers care about yield per acre and profits a lot more than my longevity. I trust the woods more.

Getting equipped for wild ricing takes some effort and money—a canoe, a push pole, knockers, and a vehicle to get it all to the lake. There is a financial barrier even for people who just want to buy wild rice, which costs more than white rice in the grocery store. But these barriers can be surmounted in many different ways. A lot of tribes and nonprofit programs have community ricing programs, in which they supply equipment and transportation and bring people to the lakes to harvest. Many also have community gardening programs and community sugarbush operations. The most important thing to do to get started is get connected and show up. Contact your tribal natural resource office or urban tribal office, or a nonprofit like the White Earth Land Recovery Project.

There is another barrier that a lot of people face when exploring our tribal harvest practices. It has nothing to do with being urban or from the reservation or having limited financial resources. It has to do with how we have been told to think about indigeneity. "Indian time" is a highly misunderstood concept. It does not mean that it's okay to be late or lazy. In former times, lazy people watched their kids go hungry. That idea is not an Indigenous concept; it's a byproduct of colonization and assimilation. Tom Stillday told me that Indian time just means you will sit here and do your ceremony for as long as it takes, with no shortcuts. Our people worked hard. They also operated with a strong belief in the value of respect. They would do everything in their power to respect other people and their time, including being on time and not making their elders wait unless it was unavoidable. I watched my elders like Melvin Eagle at ceremonies closely. Melvin was always an hour early, even if start was announced for six in the morning. He was smiling and eager to do whatever he had to do.

In our harvest practices, I think often about the teachings from a first kill feast and so many of our other ceremonies. We are communal. In former times, we harvested together and put our food together in a common food cache. Then whoever needed something took whatever they needed. We are highly influenced by the rest of the world, and the rest of the world is not communal. So, it's important that we remind ourselves to be generous with our harvest and to express gratitude through ceremony. Every major harvest includes not just offerings before the taking but a thanksgiving afterward. Each season has staple foods, and they get a special feast. In the fall it is the wild rice. In the spring it is the maple. These are the times to offer tobacco and food. When we do, we feed the spirits that watch over us, feed our relatives in the spirit world, and invite our living relatives to partake in the bounty of the season with us.

FALL CULTURE

Adults have many resources in the cultural toolbox for this unique phase of life, but the resources come with many responsibilities. It's hard to manage everything, especially when making ends meet and keeping kids alive is enough to fill most people's time to saturation. But that's exactly why leaning in to the seasonal routines and shouldering the special burden, or providing initiative for orchestrating cultural experience, is so important.

Adults have a special responsibility to younger people, too. When we live our culture and prioritize spending time on that, it shows young people how important our ceremonies and ways really are. Bear smoke and water ceremonies are spring season ceremonies, but it is people in the fall season of their lives who pull everyone together to make those things happen. Adults have to balance and engage in the harvest activities and set the cultural climate for our homes.

Winter is just around the corner, and adults need to think ahead. We usually do a fall water ceremony, much like the one in spring, to keep us safe in the winter months when fishing or traveling on the ice. We store medicines and food in anticipation of the long winter. We make offerings at the drums—to offer thanks for the harvests and to seek protection and guidance for the winter months. We never know better than the spirits what is best for us.

HEALING

Fall is a phase in people's lives when illnesses can emerge, and we need to look to the cultural toolbox not just for growth and protection and grounding but for healing as well. This is another area of our cultural patrimony where it is better to send people to their healers and elders, rather than put it all down in a book. The medicines and practices are varied and spiritually directed. But it is good for people to know a little about the types of healers we have.

In the Ojibwe language we don't really have a word for "medicine man," "medicine woman," or "shaman." We have several kinds of healers, each with a name. A nanaandawi'iwewinini is an Ojibwe doctor, and the word literally means "one who fixes." Someone with this gift often accepts tobacco and prays, prescribes traditional medicine, interprets dreams, and uses bones to pull sickness out of people. They may use eagle wing bones, hawk wing bones, or rabbit leg bones, washed and cut down. Some are boodaajigewinini, meaning they blow air through the bones to heal. Other are wiikoondawi'iwewinini, meaning they suck sickness out through the bones. It's a specialized healing gift, usually acquired through fasting, dreaming, and long apprenticeship to knowledgeable healers.

Another healing option is to seek a jiisakiiwinini, or shake tent practitioner. Someone who runs shake tent will have helpers construct a tent, just a few feet across and up to twelve feet high, covered in cloth and open at the top. The practitioner goes inside and speaks directly to the spirits. Those in need of help approach the tent from the outside and, one at a time, grab the base of one of the poles and verbalize their request. They get answers to questions only the spirits can answer—who their clan is, for example. They sometimes get Native names. And most commonly, they get healing, often followed up with specific instructions about a medicine or food offering.

In some parts of Ojibwe country there are people who practice bear walking, a shape-shifting practice that enables the practitioner to travel in bear form and deliver healing to those who request it. Some think it's just a bunch of superstitious nonsense. Others truly fear the bear walkers, who have been treated with suspicion and fear that they might use their powers to harm rather than help.

When in need of healing and help, we often put out bowls of

food and do a simple pipe ceremony. We may bring bowls of food to the ceremonial drums, where anyone's food and tobacco can be offered as a special request and attached to the group's prayer at the ceremony. When dealing with trauma or guided by profound signs, people seek initiation into the medicine dance. For that, people need to seek lodge chiefs for guidance.

Margaret Treuer. ***Anton Treuer***

WINTER
Elderhood

My mother, Margaret "Peggy" Treuer, used to call following our ways "walking the Red Road." Walking that road my entire life has always led me to look for signs. The dream that Archie Mosay had about me changed both of our lives and led me to commit my life's work to helping others find the Red Road. The vision I had when I went fasting as a young man deepened and amplified my sense of purpose in this world. Signs can help us find our way. For me, a great revelation came when I was touched by winter's hand: the signs that help us find our way are not always dreams and visions and signs from nature. They can be people.

The people who have been my signposts and guides have often been elders, whose winter wisdom illuminated the path.

Archie had a dream about me that inspired his faith in me, and that inspired my faith in myself. But it was my relationship with him, and my showing up to live the culture with him, that really changed my course. How ironic then, as venerated as Ojibwe elders are and as strongly as I relied on my elders, that my deepest understanding of elderhood was sparked by one of the youngest humans in my life: my daughter Mia Treuer.

Mia is twelve years old now. She has bright brown eyes and olive skin. She is so sweet and kind and accommodating that people are sometimes taken by surprise to see how incredibly confident, self-assured, and assertive she can be when she feels the need. She doesn't occupy a lot of air space. She just acts, like when she mastered all of the curriculum for third grade by the end of the first month of the school year and had to get bumped up a grade. She seems to have control of her life. It would be completely intimidating if she weren't so humble, to the point of shyness, about her remarkable brain and spiritual insight.

When I was Mia's age, I never felt in control of anything in my life. I have fond memories of those years. I grew up in the little cabin that I escaped to after the failure of my marriage to Elias's mother. It had kerosene lanterns and an outhouse in those days. But we spent our summers picking pin cherries, plums, blueberries, and raspberries. We washed up at the river or area lakes, which meant swimming every day. My mother was my Red Road in those days—showing us how to tap maple trees and snare rabbits, and dragging us to many different kinds of ceremonies. It must have been hard for my mom at times, but as a twelve-year-old boy, I had all I ever wanted. My brother David and I built forts and dug trenches across the dirt road in front of our house to mess with the cars whizzing by, sometimes to dramatic effect.

My mother went through big transitions in those years. She had recently become the first female Native attorney in the state

Mom as a new lawyer—the first female Native attorney in Minnesota.
Robert Treuer

of Minnesota. It was so inspiring to me to see her step into the courtroom with her Indian Health Service Coke-bottle eyeglasses, powwow braids, and Sorel boots and stand up to the people and institutions of white power. She launched a remarkable career, but for the rest of my childhood, she had a lot less time for berry picking. I remember her building clients for her private law practice. She took payment in walleye and wild rice from a lot of her Native clients. Eventually, the financial rewards started to grow, and she built a big, beautiful home for her family just on the other side of a five-acre pond from the cabin we had called home for years.

Her relationship with my dad had a traumatic test at that time, too. They kept the details from their kids, as parents often do, but my mom moved out for three months. After she came back, she seemed emotionally distant from all of us for years. They divorced several years later, when the last of my siblings was finishing high school, but the emotional separation happened when I was still in middle school. As a kid, I found my father's transgressions and my mother's reaction both baffling and painful. Although boys often pull away from their mothers as a natural part of maturing and finding independence when they become teenagers, it felt like more than that to me. She was emotionally distant when I wanted her close. As a preteen and teenager, I had to learn how to rely on other parts of our cultural village to nourish my needs. I poured myself into school, friends, hunting, and fishing. It was hard for me to find the same depth of connection with my mom, who retreated to her work, books, and television. I was busy, too—finishing high school, college, and graduate school, spending countless hours at ceremonies, and traveling all over Ojibwe country, then starting a family, restarting, and raising children.

There were signs along the way pointing me back to my mom. Her battle with lung cancer was one. I was at her house with my pipe, outside the surgery door with tobacco, by her side for ceremonies afterward. And she beat it—cancer free for over a decade. That experience echoed a decade later, when she got pancreatic cancer: more ceremonies, more food offerings, and more luck. She beat that, too, and never got cancer again. But nothing was the same. She needed oxygen day and night. She was still in the world and able to laugh and watch her grandchildren, but she was frail now. She tired easily.

My mother had been my cultural anchor, Red Road coach, and recreational companion for the first twelve years of my life. Neither one of us knew it would be this way at the time, but she never reclaimed those roles in my life. The reasons were understandable, but it was still painful. I missed her.

My mother's declining health left me feeling powerless. In many ways that's exactly what we all are when it comes to facing the mortality of our loved ones. Any power I *felt* before that was just imagined.

I own my share of the distance between my mother and me. I was so busy trying to provide for my kids and revitalize our language that it was hard for anyone to keep up with me. My mother never lacked ambition, but she wasn't born in a hurry-up time. I've come to realize, too, that I was mad at her. I was a little resentful that she never reasserted herself at the center of my childhood, the way she had when I was little. But I was really upset that she smoked cigarettes, right through two cancer battles and even with chronic obstructive pulmonary disease, COPD. The spirits had given her new leases on life, but she was shortening her time and further reducing her ability to be physically and mentally present with her family because of her limited lung function.

I routinely picked up my mom's medications and brought her to appointments. She needed me and my sister Megan now and relied on us for this help. We started to serve as intermediaries with her doctors, since she was often tired and forgot important details.

Mia Treuer. ***Blair Treuer***

When they told us that there was only an 18 percent chance that she would be alive three years later, it finally felt real. After getting her settled at her house, I warmed up my car and drove down the road a mile or so, pulled over, and cried. I would lose her—there was no way around that. But losing the closeness between us that had sustained me throughout my childhood seemed like a needless sacrifice. I just couldn't see a way to overcome her fatigue, much less all the time that had passed, to make things like they were.

The kids were LARPing (live-action role-playing) when I got home—fighting epic battles with foam weapons in the snow outside our house. I changed into my snow bibs and smacked them with LARP weapons for a few minutes before making everyone load up to haul sap in the sugarbush. My truck pulls a trailer with a three-hundred-gallon water drum, and we filled it up. When we got home after all the playing and chores, the kids were exhausted. They all went inside to snack and rest. Mia was the sole exception. She was staring at me next to the truck, her bright brown eyes seeing more than they should have been able to.

"What's wrong, Dad?"

"Everything is okay," I replied. "I'm just worried about Grandma Peggy."

She kept staring and asked, "Can you take me to see her?" I nodded. "Just a minute," she said, and she scurried to the garage and came back with a pouch of tobacco I had left on the workbench and an ax. "For Grandma," she said, as she opened the tobacco and put a pinch in my hand. We put tobacco by the pine tree, said a short prayer, and drove to her house. I couldn't help but wonder whether that kid brought the ax for the firewood we'd be splitting or if it was a reminder of what it meant in our cultural toolbox.

After that, Mia was in my ear often asking to go see her grandma. She wanted to bake cookies at her house. She wanted to watch football with her. She wanted to watch movies. My mom knew how to play her grandkids, too. She kept popsicles, candy, and cookies in ample quantities. She had a fully loaded entertainment system and big, fluffy pillows to lounge on while watching television. Mia knew that Grandma's house was small and couldn't handle all of us all the time, so she timed her requests perfectly to force me to take her. And she was always easier company at my mom's because she wasn't trying to start a LARP war in the house, which her brothers simply could not stop doing. But part of me wonders whether that little twelve-year-old kid was orchestrating all that time at Grandma Peggy's for herself, for her grandmother, or for me. The spirits have a lot of ways to get things done.

My mom did get tired easily, but she was still a fireball. Mia liked it when she talked about politics because my mother could not talk about Donald Trump without cursing. The cursing made me want to go cover Mia's ears, because my mother was gifted at the art, as only a rez girl straight out of Bena can be. But Mia just giggled at her political tirades and my discomfort with the cursing.

As I was prepping food for my mother and daughter, doing the dishes, watching television shows, and talking politics, my mother started to share stories with me that I had never heard. There were stories about her childhood, her marriage to my dad, another boyfriend before him who wanted to get married. She asked me to help her with paperwork—deeds, retirement accounts, her will, and funeral instructions. She forbade me to officiate any part of her send-off, even though I had been officiating at funerals for years: "You can help other families when their loved ones change worlds. When I go, you have to focus on your own grief and the needs of your family." She didn't leave much to chance.

The long hours together seemed to thaw the ice between us, and my mother and I had a lot more heart-to-heart talks. I told her everything I had been feeling, and the pain seemed to evaporate when we shined some light on it. She explained that she didn't have a lot of examples of what healthy relationships, healthy parenting, or even healthy communication looked like. But she was so glad that we were talking now. I came to realize that I didn't need my mom to be what she had been when I was twelve—architect of my life and constant companion. I just needed to know that I was loved that deeply all along. And I was. A warm, peaceful understanding flowed between us. I feel it still.

My mom proved the doctors wrong one last time. We held that state longer than the three years they thought she'd have, but not forever. We moved her to Megan's house when her time got short. Mia and her siblings came with me often. We sang her Ojibwe songs and fed her the last food she'd be able to take—chocolate pudding. She woke up once after that to ask for her bundle of sacred items and held them close in her soft, leathery hands until she pulled her last breath. My brother Micah shut off her oxygen machine. Peace.

As I reflect on those last few years of my mother's life, I'm not sure who was helping who. At the time, I thought I was being a good, dutiful son, helping his mom in her old age. But I was being schooled by my twelve-year-old daughter in the importance of forgiveness, communication, and the power of just showing up. And through all the paperwork, conversations, chores, and tobacco offerings, my mom taught me how to navigate the winter—our season of aging and dying, peace and wisdom. What a gift they have given.

RESPECT FOR ELDERS

Our word for elder, *gichi-aya'aa*, means "great being." Our word for elder woman, *mindimooye*, means "one who holds us together" and describes the role of the family matriarch. You don't have to say "respect your elders" when you're operating in Ojibwe; every word used to talk about them is loaded with respect. Each of the four stages of life (infancy, youth, adulthood, and old age) is beautiful.

The goal is not to stay twenty forever, or to fight wrinkles and gray hair with Botox injections, face-lifts, and hair dye. The cultural toolbox teaches us to look forward to all stages of life.

We have a saying in Ojibwe: "Apegish ge-bimaadiziyan biinish gashkitoosiwan geyaabi ji-zhaashaagamikawad miskomin." It means "I hope that you live to be so old that you can't even crush a raspberry between your gums." It's considered a blessing. We have a custom, too, when someone does a good deed for an elder. The elder may touch their own head and then touch the head of the young person and say, "Waabikwaan bezhig gimiinin." It means "I'm giving you a white hair." It's a way of saying that the goal is to live a long life and get to the point where you have a full head of white hair. You get there one good deed at a time.

People who have lived a long time know things. They are smart and wise and experienced. They have perspective on their lives and the world around them. We all learn a lot from our elders. At both ceremonial and social functions, our elders eat first. When many knowledgeable culture carriers gather together, deference is customarily given to the host community or family and to the eldest culture keeper from that group who is present to speak for everyone gathered.

I always admired Archie Mosay in his elder years. Everyone wanted to know what he knew and relied on him to get them through ceremonies. He lived alone most of the time, but his kids were always nearby. His daughter Dora Ammann often came over to cook and clean. His son Dan Mosay mowed the grass. He had lots of people in his life, but he was independent, too. The older he got, the more important he became.

Only ten thousand years ago, all humans all over the planet were tribal and Indigenous. We all had earth-based worldviews and communal ways of structuring our societies. It's different for most people now, and one of the things lost for many is the intergenerational transmission of cultural knowledge. Often, important cultural knowledge is filtered and administered by a church, synagogue, or educational institution. One of the casualties is a devaluing of elders. The modern world is pretty ageist. We separate people by age—first graders with first graders, adults with adults, and elders with elders. Rebuilding intergenerational connection and transmission of knowledge is a powerful, decolonizing, and healing effort.

My namesake the late Mary Roberts gave me a great teaching about our responsibility to share our culture. She told me that whenever I learn something from the cultural toolbox—a word in our language, a song, a medicine, how to do a ceremony—I should make sure to teach it to at least four other people. If we all do that, those words, songs, medicines, and ceremonies keep going. We should strive to be replaceable four times over in everything we do with the cultural toolbox. I try to do that, and it keeps me leaning in when I have moments of doubt. Seeing my students teaching our language and my apprentices at ceremony starting to officiate is beyond gratifying. It gives me hope that seven generations from now, when nobody remembers my name, our cultural toolbox will still be available to my descendants.

HEALING REVISITED

I've explained major healing practices in earlier sections of this book. As we enter elderhood, we eventually develop health problems and need more help. A lot of elders end up using traditional medicines routinely to regulate blood pressure, deal with clogged arteries and moderate digestive issues, and treat chronic pain. Our woods hold a vast array of medicines, and quite a few people know about them. The medicines we have and the ceremonies we use to prescribe and administer them can address all kinds of healing—physical ailments and diseases, but emotional traumas, depression, and anxiety, too. If we live a long time, most of us have to grapple with some of these.

It's sometimes difficult to know how to balance our legitimate concerns about the modern medical world with its benefits and integrate that with our cultural toolbox. In 1492, Natives had a rich store of medicines and cultural knowledge. The diseases brought by Europeans still killed about 95 percent of us. The cultural toolbox is powerful, but not a panacea. At the same time, it's hard to trust the government and the health profession. The Indian Health Service, run by the US federal government, sterilized seventy-five thousand Native women without their consent in the 1960s and 1970s. There is a medical industrial complex running modern medicine, and it seems to care about selling its products a lot more than anyone's longevity. I try to be as informed as possible about what the modern medical world has to offer. I try to make decisions based on common sense and logic. I get blood tests and vaccinations. I saw major invasive surgeries save my mother's life twice. The modern medical world does have something to offer; I go to my cultural toolbox first for many things, but I use the modern medical world as well. When the COVID-19 pandemic hit, we prayed and made food offerings, and we hung medicine in our house. We also listened to sensible advice. I taught my classes on Zoom, we pulled the kids from school, and we had groceries delivered so we could distance from others. As soon as vaccines were available, our entire crew got them. And we required vaccination for people coming to ceremony because we have an ethical responsibility not to convene a gathering that might get someone killed.

HISTORICAL TRAUMA

As we get older, we usually gain perspective on different kinds of injury and healing. We are products of our own good and bad choices and good and bad luck, but we are also products of our gene pool and its epigenetic blessings and curses. Many call the curses historical trauma.

The Ojibwe have talked about historical trauma in our own terms for a long time. When we frame knowledge, belonging, connection, and culture in terms of seven generations, this is what we mean. What happens to us now, good or bad, will reverberate seven generations into the future. And how we are now is a product of seven generations of development, passed on not just through learned knowledge but through our very DNA.

The scientists now working on historical trauma and epigenetics (the study of how behaviors and the environment can cause changes that affect the way your genes work, and how those changes can be inherited) are finally starting to catch up with our elders. Mice who are subjected to a pain stimulus at the same time they smell a certain chemical will fear that smell. Scientists at Emory University showed that their offspring, for two generations, will also fear it, even if they have never experienced the pain stimulus. Other studies have looked at the health and longevity of men held in Civil War prisons, descendants of Holocaust survivors, and people who survived a famine; the children of all had bad health outcomes. We inherit triggers and don't always know why something is triggering our behavior in a certain way. Schoolteachers, bankers, government officials—all trying to help—might be hitting an epigenetic response with us and not even know it.

The Adverse Childhood Experiences Study, carried out since the 1990s by the Centers for Disease Control and Kaiser Permanente, has shown that if someone has five adverse childhood experiences (abuses or traumas), their brains get rewired. The thinking part of our brains (prefrontal cortex) goes offline so we can fight, flee, or freeze. A little experience with that is actually good for us. But too much of it, too intensely, keeps our prefrontal cortex from running the show. We fight people in positions of power when we don't need to. We even fight family members. Or we flee from trouble and even from healthy relationships. Or we space out, zone out, and disengage.

Healing from these things is no simple process. We need to rewire our brains. Luckily, the cultural toolbox helps. And the older we get, the better our chances of wrangling the demons that plague us all. The protocols for a lot of our ceremonies are grounding routines. For example, we move in a clockwise direction for most ceremonies, even when it's not exactly convenient. The repeated circles around the food at naming ceremonies and around the drum at ceremonial drums let us drop off our traumas a little at a time. The cyclical water ceremonies, bear smokes, and moon ceremonies help purge and heal—not just in the moment, but in an accumulating catharsis that amplifies as we age.

We all need healing. And we need healing places to go. Our ceremonial life offers many options. When we come to the wigwam or the sweat lodge, the powwow arena or the ceremonial drum dance hall, we can find affinity space with our fellow humans trying to walk the Red Road. We can take off a layer of the armor that so many of us wear when we travel the world where other cultures dominate. We can just be.

A lot of us have been disconnected from the cultural toolbox through no fault of our own. That's not fair. But if we wait for fairness to come to us, we will likely be terribly disappointed. It is better to make our own luck. Seeking out the people who are seeking a cultural life, and the places where the culture lives, will serve us well. In urban and reservation spaces alike, we may have to take the initiative to pursue those people and places, but it's well worth it.

As we spend more and more time over our lives in our cultural environments, that culture rubs off on us. The burden lightens. We can see and place our pains in better context. Remember that while historical and contemporary traumas get passed on to us and to future generations, the good stuff gets inherited and passed forward, too. We are the humans in the history of humans who figured out how to get along, how to build things, how to get enough food when it's cold out there and the ground is covered in snow. We are resilient, strong, and beautiful individuals who have inherited a remarkable cultural patrimony and toolbox for healing.

LAUGHTER IS MEDICINE

The Ojibwe have a notorious sense of humor. When people ask why, we sometimes say, "It's the trauma"; that answer sounds funny to most Ojibwe people but doesn't land with everyone else the same way. Sometimes laughing is all you can do. But laughter is healing. And Ojibwe people like to tease—it shows affinity. We have nicknames for one another that are often anything but flattering. When someone farts, someone else is likely to say "Gidizhinikaaz," meaning "Your name is." We have whole genres of jokes about Indigenous poverty and unemployment (we're better lovers if we don't have to get up and go to work in the morning). We even laugh at funerals. We grieve there, too, but it rarely feels like a solemn affair when we send someone off. Our language naturally lends itself to humor and plays on words.

It's healthy for us to laugh at ourselves and not take ourselves too seriously. Mary Roberts liked to say that white people have imaginations, but we have visions. They can show up in surprising ways. My friend David Roy was once having car trouble (which happened a lot of times), and he opened the hood to consult with six or seven of us well-wishing wannabe mechanics. I'm not making this up: he had at least a dozen different kinds of Ojibwe medicine under the hood. A root tied to his carburetor. Tobacco tie attached to the fuel line. A bundle of sage fastened with yarn to the oil pan. A little bag of medicine in leaf form tied to the battery cable. David clearly had a very different idea of how to go about being a mechanic than I did. We all stared at everything for a few minutes, not wanting to offend him. Finally, I said, "Talk about running on a prayer!" Everyone burst out laughing, slapping their knees and teasing him for about twenty minutes. He got mad and stomped away, which just made everyone laugh harder. He came sulking back after a while, and we tried to lean in to giving some real mechanical advice, but someone started giggling every couple of minutes, and the teasing started all over again. We actually did fix that car. It just took a couple hours because of all the shenanigans and teasing. David thanked everyone and then declared, "You guys can't say that my medicines didn't keep this pony running as long as it did." He really meant that, and I suppose we can't really prove him wrong. But we were all laughing again, and he joined right in after that.

One time, the FedEx guy delivered a package to our sweat lodge instead of to the house. The sweat lodge is located half a mile away, and there are no other buildings by it. I'm real proud of our sweat lodge, but we had so many questions. Did he drop it off and think, "Those poor people"? Did he go to the house first and think, "Hell no, that's too run-down to be the delivery site"? Did the sweat look like a more likely place to be the order-and-delivery location? Did he think we had internet service in that sweat? We still laugh every time it comes up. I actually had to convince Blair not to go to the office and chew them out, but I really wanted her to do it so I could record the whole conversation for laughs. I told her the delivery guy might not be the one you want delivering the packages, but he would definitely be the best company to take out to dinner.

The company of my fellow Natives is a great respite from the ways of the rest of the world. Burdens halve and joys double. I do think it's wise for us to check ourselves, too, so that our mirth doesn't come at the expense of someone else's self-esteem—even if we naturally push those boundaries from time to time.

DEATH

The funeral rite is one of those areas of sacred knowledge that is somewhat guarded in the Ojibwe world. We give instructions to the souls of the departing at funerals but don't share them outside of that context, even with apprentices who are learning the rite. It would be like sending off someone who is still with us. So, I can't provide a how-to list for funeral ceremonies. But death happens to us all, and anyone lucky enough to live a while will lose loved ones. Understanding the Ojibwe worldview on death is a critical piece of the cultural toolbox.

We don't have souls. We *are* souls. We have bodies—for a little while. We are not humans looking for a spiritual experience. We are spirits having a temporary human experience.

Death is not an end. It is a change. In our creation story, we were made out of a clump of dirt. We were infused with a unique light, breath, and sound. So, when we die, our bodies go back to the earth. But our unique light, breath, and sound go on. Those things constitute our souls. When we pass away, the souls change worlds.

It wasn't always this way. We have a story about two creations—a first creation and a second one, before and after the great flood. We were mortal in the first creation, but in the second creation we were immortal. We did not experience death. There is a legend we tell at wakes about Wenabozho, who had helped in the re-creation after the flood and grew upset that he wasn't getting enough tobacco and food offerings. I'll save the details for the wakes, but he eventually went searching for help to teach us a lesson. Though he intended to give a lesson and nothing more, he made a mistake and broke the spell of everlasting life. We became mortal.

What goes around comes around. Wenabozho soon became the first person to experience the loss of a loved one, whose soul now blew when the wind blew. Wenabozho grieved and destroyed things, but he eventually recovered himself and directed his relative's spirit on a journey to the place of never-ending happiness. He made the road of souls we all follow when we die.

At wakes, everyone shares a tobacco offering with the deceased and eats with them. The officiating crew shares these and other legends in full detail and charges up the spirit of the deceased with our ceremonial music. At the funeral, the tobacco and food process is repeated and then the head officiant gives instructions to the departing soul on how to get to the spirit world. The head officiant also gives instructions to the bereaved on how to deal with grief. There are more songs and a past review (where everyone comes up to view the body of the departing one last time), and the spirit of the deceased is on its way before the body is interred.

Young children and pregnant women usually don't attend wakes and funerals while the body of the deceased is present, or they stay back from the casket if attendance is unavoidable. Both are discouraged from participating in the past review. If a child comes to a wake, they wear a smudge of charcoal on the forehead to serve as a pass-over—so the departing soul won't take the kid with or give them nightmares. We usually cover mirrors in the building, and people take off their glasses when they come to look at the body. The spirit of the deceased is looking at them, too, and seeing their reflection can be upsetting to the departing spirit. We tell people not to drop tears on the body or it might make for a misty or rainy journey for them. People are encouraged to hug the living if they need to cry.

The family does many things to prepare for a funeral, but that to-do list is part of their ceremony instructions, so I won't share the details here. Everything is for the departing, to ease their journey to the next world. A fire is kept going, day and night, from the time of passing until the end of the funeral.

If someone died and had no funeral at all, their spirit would still separate from their body and find its way to the spirit world.

Before the middle of the 1800s, when the Ojibwe went to war and someone fell in battle, their comrades left them there or propped up their body up facing their enemies and went home with full confidence that they would make it to the spirit world. The entire funeral process we use now provides legends for the soul to understand its transformation (separating from its body), music to empower the departing spirit, instructions to guide the spirit, and procedures to give the soul a little push in the right direction. It's an important ceremony and not one to mess around with haphazardly. But the soul won't be stuck without it.

We do not have a concept of heaven and hell. All departing souls go to the same place. Our character, choices, and deeds on earth have no impact on that. There is no judgment after death, and there is no word for *sin* in Ojibwe. We can behave or misbehave, do good or bad deeds, but none condemn or save our souls. We just journey on.

The spirit of the deceased is emotionally attached to its body, so in many places, a small hole is drilled in the casket and rough box. Burials are often only four feet deep, rather than six. In many places, a spirit house is built over the grave site with a little hole in the end. The holes in the spirit house, rough box, and casket allow the spirit to visit its interred body after arriving in the spirit world. In former times, the spirit houses used to be miniature wigwams. They are maintained for only four years, and then they are allowed to go back to nature—to decay and collapse. In some places people don't use spirit houses at all. Whether they do or don't has no spiritual effect; spirit houses are for the family left behind to honor and feed their relative, more than for the deceased. Nobody needs the house just to send food to the spirit world. My family uses spirit houses for our loved ones. My mom's is built out of cedar and unpainted. Some people use pine boards and paint them. The orientation of the body varies a bit by community. In many places, the head is in the west, but at Red Lake all bodies are oriented facing the lake, no matter what side of it they are buried on.

The traditional custom is to bury, rather than cremate. Because the departing soul is emotionally attached to its body, this allows for a slow, natural return to earth. Cremation is viewed as abrupt. Embalming is new, and some families refuse to embalm. There can be challenges with the legal system; autopsies are sometimes required by law when there is a homicide or when ordered by a medical examiner, but when they aren't required, usually people avoid them, even if the cause of death is not entirely certain. One Sandy Lake family had to resist autopsies in two generations. They took their relative's body from the funeral home to avoid an autopsy and ended up being chased by the police in the first case. The second time, they got lawyers involved and fought it out.

If someone has an amputation during their life, the amputated limb is buried after the surgery with no ceremony required. It is not saved so it can be placed in the casket with someone when they die. Once it is separated from the body, it is viewed like hair or fingernail trimmings, which don't serve a continuing spiritual function.

When I officiate or help at a funeral, I make a tea out of cedar when I get home. I drink a cup of the tea and pour some on a washcloth and wash my hands and face with it. It helps cleanse the death vibes. I try to do that before I start hugging up the kids. Their intuition is more naturally sensitive than adults'. Failing to do the cedar wash and tea won't hurt them, but they might be a little disturbed or have trouble sleeping. It helps me get grounded in my home space and other life pursuits as well.

FEEDING THE DEAD

We don't really die; we change worlds. The spirit world is often called the place of everlasting happiness. Our ancestors through all the generations are there. They sleep, visit, cook, and eat. They are more ethereal, having been without bodies, without physical forms, since they passed. So, we take responsibility here on earth for nourishing them in our own way. We feed the dead.

We have many ways to feed the dead. At wakes and funerals there are two primary ways we do this. The northern way, seen always at Red Lake and in Canada and many other places, is to use the fire to send food to the spirit world. Usually, we make a spirit plate, with a sample of each food item at the feast, and burn it with tobacco in the fire. In Red Lake, each person at the funeral puts a piece of each food item on their plate in a box and the whole thing is burned. The fire is like a doorway that can be used to transport the food to the spirit world and transform it into a form most easily consumed by the spirits of the dead.

The southern way of feeding the dead at wakes and funerals, used across Wisconsin, at Mille Lacs, and in many other places, is to place a bowl or bowls of food in front of the casket and have close family members eat the spirit food on behalf of the departing soul. Because of their emotional and spiritual affinity with the departing, this serves to nourish the spirit of the deceased.

When we are not at wakes and funerals, we still feed relatives in the spirit world. Some people do this at all of their ceremonies, as a matter of regular protocol. Those who prepare a spirit dish at other ceremonies or even at home can burn it in the fire or leave it in a clean place outside—on a tree branch, on the ground, or in the water. In the southern custom, someone blesses a bowl of food which is then eaten by relatives of the deceased. People even bring spirit bowls to ceremonial drums and other ceremonies and send on the food there. The spirits of the dead can be fed anytime, although in some places it is done customarily during the night, since nighttime is daytime in the spirit world and vice versa.

GRIEVING

Dealing with grief can be really hard, but our toolbox has carried me through some of the toughest times in my life. The teachings range from how to think of the loss to what to do with the grief.

In Ojibwe there is no word for *goodbye*. (The English word *goodbye* actually comes from "God be with you.") In life and death, we use phrases such as "Giga-waabamin miinawaa," meaning "I'll see you again." This asserts the soul-to-soul connection between two people—in this world or the next, I will see you again. The guidance on death, discussed above, sets a frame to help us grapple with the loss. Only the body of our loved one goes in the ground. Their soul lives on and travels to another plane of existence. Thinking of the departing soul as an ever-living spirit rather than as the body that spirit inhabited helps with healthy detachment and acceptance. We tell people that even if they live one hundred years on earth, it is but a drop of water in the rushing stream of time that they will eventually get to share with their relative when their time comes. We also tell people to do their best to live a long time. It would be the wish of their departing relative that they have long, healthy, happy lives. And the best way to honor their relative is to live a long time and remember them.

Our suffering is in this world, not the next. Every step of someone's journey to the spirit world drops off sickness, pain, and suffering; every step makes the soul lighter and less burdened. We typically do not wear black at funerals. There is no clothing requirement, but often people wear brightly colored clothing. We are encouraged to visit and laugh during the meals and when someone is not in the middle of officiating. We can be happy that struggle and suffering is over for the departing. This is easier to accept for someone who faced a long illness than for someone who died unexpectedly or very young, but even for those who go early, the pain and trauma is left behind.

At the end of the departing person's journey, they will be reunited with their loved ones—it will be a happy family reunion. We tell people to think about how happy their loved one will be to see them. We also send food to the departing person for their spirit to share with all their relatives when they arrive.

People often feel loss and even abandonment when a relative passes away. We tell them they are not alone. This is a loss for all of us, and we share in their grief, even if our pain is not as intense as that of the immediate family.

We tell people to remember to use tobacco. When Wenabozho—the first person to experience a death—was grieving, his grief was so powerful that he couldn't think, and everything he touched was ruined. He wilted grass, shattered rocks, and splintered trees. But when Wenabozho put down tobacco, he was able to release his grief a little at a time. So, the grieving are encouraged to put tobacco by the rocks and trees and in the water. It doesn't make the grief go away, but it helps to lessen its weight.

We encourage people to seek out veterans. Those who have faced death this way have a special wisdom and can help to counsel us in our time of loss. Talking to them helps release the grief, too, and can help us go forward in our own lives.

We tell the grieving about our medicines. There is a tea they can make from the bark of a poplar tree to help ease and discharge the grief. We use cedar in a similar way—as a tea, as a wash, or even in the bathtub for a regular bath.

We tell people to get up in the morning. Our spirits are strong in the morning, and the sun has the power to help dry our tears and warm our bodies and spirits. It's easier to see. One of our words for sadness is *gashkendam*, which literally means "to have foggy or clouded emotions." The sun can burn the fog away, a little at a time. It also keeps our awake time in the realm of the living as much as possible and reduces obsessing on our loss.

We explain that since grief is very powerful, it can affect a wild rice crop or a hunter's luck. So, much as we do at a first kill feast or during a young woman's first year as a woman, the most immediately bereaved will abstain from all traditional foods after they are first harvested until they can be fed by having the food offered four times before eating. This removes some of the grief and the possibility that the grief will affect the harvest or abundance of a traditional food.

The most immediately bereaved also refrain from touching brand-new babies or puppies—any kind of new life—until they have completed their period of mourning, which lasts one year. They can use gloves and cedar to protect sacred items and new life that they cannot avoid coming close to until their mourning is over.

We tell people to put away their pictures of their loved one and think of them not as the physical form they saw every day but as the spiritual form they are now. After one year, the pictures come out and can be copied and shared freely. We also tell people to give away the clothes of the deceased. Their sacred items can be kept in the family, but their everyday items should be given away. In Red Lake this is done one year after the loss. In most other places it is done as soon as possible after the funeral.

We tell people that their lives have been rearranged. They should not leave the room of the deceased as it was or set up an altar to their remembrance. They should rearrange the furniture in their house. And they should accept that they will have to rearrange their lives. It is part of acceptance and letting go.

We tell people that the spirits love them and will watch them closely during the first year after their loss. How they handle themselves sets a pattern for how their lives will go. They should be kind to one another. They should seek out one another to visit and socialize. It will help the family members be close to one another.

We tell people not to drown their grief in drugs, alcohol, gambling, or anything else addictive.

We tell people that their departing relative loves them as much as they love their relative. They have to show that they are okay enough that their relative doesn't have to stick around and take care of them. To this end, they are encouraged to hug the living when they need to cry rather than crowding the casket at a funeral. We even place a veil over the casket at wakes and funerals to help people emotionally detach from the physical form of their loved one and release their spirit to the spirit world.

There is no magic pill or quick ceremony for grieving. There is no way around it; there is just a way through it. So, we tell people to go through it. When they pick up their cultural toolbox, it will help them. Every time there is a ceremony, the pipe smoke will help waft away their hurt. And it will help bond them to the earth and their fellow humans here on earth.

In our area, it is customary for a grieving family to also approach the ceremonial drums for help. A long time ago, when people were grieving, they rubbed charcoal on their faces and left their hair unbraided, so as to avoid showing vanity or pride. When the first ceremonial drum came to the Anishinaabe, it was a gift from the Dakota, who came back to check on us and make sure we were keeping the tradition alive. The first man seated as a drum chief experienced a terrible loss—the death of his son. He said the drum was evil and the Dakota were evil, too. His face was black with charcoal and his hair was wild and unbraided. He got up to leave, but the Dakota stopped him. They took him by the hand, gently led him around the drum, and seated him again. They carefully washed the charcoal from his face and combed and braided his hair. They gave him fresh clothes to wear. Then they piled up gifts in front of him, begging him to go on with life and go on with the drum. The Dakota warriors present used special songs, and, one at a time, four of the warriors danced around the drum and then danced around the man and wiped his falling tears. Each warrior left a red mark on the man's face where the tears had been. Then they lifted him to his feet and sang a fifth song, bringing him back into the arena to dance around the drum, symbolizing his continuation of living. Today, people usually don't use charcoal the same way or even leave their hair unbraided. But we replicate that ceremony for each family when they have a loss. We take them by the hands and walk them around the drum, wash their faces, comb and rebraid their hair. We give them gifts. We have our veterans dance around the drum and each of the family members, wipe their tears, and mark them red; when this is done, the veterans stand them up to be danced back into the circle.

This ceremony, sometimes called wiping the tears, washing the tears, or in Ojibwe wezhi'aa (fixing or decorating someone), is still practiced by the Dakota, with whom it originated. And in Ojibwe country, it happens at ceremonial drums most commonly, but sometimes separate from the drums, too. Rosemarie DeBungie, an elder from Ponemah, has done these with an open invitation for those who need healing, not just from the recent loss of a loved one but from the accumulated effects of historical and contemporary trauma.

WINTER HARVEST

Ojibwe food production is most intense in the fall, but it happens during every season, including winter. We fish hook and line through the ice. We use fish houses or tarps over larger holes and use decoys to spear. We net under the ice—which is a special skill set all by itself.

Grouse and rabbits are good hunting in the early winter, and rabbits are good snaring all winter long. February is sometimes called the stingy moon because there is often a big cold snap, and

Showing Mia how to process a rabbit. ***Caleb Treuer***

the owls come south and eat up a lot of the small game. In former times, the unprepared faced food shortages.

Winter is trapping time, too. Furs are thickest for those who trap to sell. And when the ice is thick, it's easy to see where the beavers cache their food and set traps under the ice, braced between saplings.

It's less common now, but the Ojibwe used to snare large game, too, including whitetail deer. This was done in February, after the bucks lose their horns. In most places, the tribes have stopped the practice because the does are pregnant then, and the deer get skinny with their own food scarcity issues in winter.

One of my cousins, Robert "Bobby" Matthews, spent his whole life harvesting as his only means of supporting his family. He never had a regular job; he harvested everything in our seasonal round. In the spring he made maple syrup, keeping some and selling more. He harvested leeches and minnows in the summer and sold them for bait. He also harvested pine cones and sold them to the Department of Natural Resources for seedling production—it sounds cute, but he made at least $10,000 every year doing that activity alone. He hunted in the fall and harvested wild rice by the thousands of pounds. He kept some of his rice and sold the rest. In the winter he trapped. He ran a major line and knew (or maybe invented) every trick in the book. He used to run his line with a snowmobile, and wherever he had a set he would put a pole up with an orange tag on top. If the tag was up, no kill; if it was down, he went to check. He was a hard worker. His full-time tribal harvester business brought in over $100,000 a year. He used to post pictures of beautiful northern Minnesota landscapes to Facebook and caption them "My office today." Bobby passed away in 2019, but his work ethic and cultural knowledge remain an inspiration to all who knew him.

WINTER CULTURE

Winter was the only season when old-time Ojibwe people had a long break in the constant harvest pressure, so we had a number of wintertime leisure activities. Bagese games were common in the evenings. Snow snake races were common during the day for younger people. Snow snakes are straight wooden replicas of snakes, and they are raced in snow tracks—kind of like an Ojibwe version of curling.

Winter is also the season of storytelling. Many birds and some animals have migrated out of the area. Many other animals are hibernating, or at least sleeping longer. The lakes are frozen and the turtles and frogs dormant. There is a calm, as many forms of life are resting and waiting for the burst of spring energy. The Ojibwe worried about offending other people, spirits, and creatures. But with many life forms absent or sleeping and not listening, it was acceptable to tell their stories. It is taboo to tell winter legends in any other season. In a practical sense, there was no other time of the year when people could devote so much time to the effort, so storytelling naturally settled as a winter routine and custom. But the spiritual reasons are clear, too.

The taboo only applies to winter legends. For the most part, these are the Ojibwe equivalent of *Aesop's Fables*—stories about how the rabbit got long ears, how the bear got a short tail, how the chipmunk got his stripes, and how the racoon got his eye patches. They are usually entertaining but have cultural lessons built in—cautionary tales about provoking others, excessive pride, and doubting other creatures. Many winter legends feature Wenabozho. Wenabozho was a force for good who often erred or played tricks or was led astray by his ego. Some Wenabozho stories are told as part of ceremonies any time of the year. His presence in a tale isn't a perfect barometer for determining whether a story is a winter legend. When in doubt, ask authentic storytellers, and they can clarify what's taboo and out of season and what's not. Winter legends are somewhat sacred because they share teachings and are governed by this seasonal taboo, but they are often raucous and crude in content. Wenabozho's anus, for example, is a regular feature in many of them.

THE BREATH OF THE BEAR

Nancy Jones taught me that bear cubs are born in the winter, during a six-week window of time between mid-January and the end of February. On the day they are born, the weather warms up and there is a fog—in the middle of the winter. The fog is the "breath of the bear," waking up the bear cubs. A lot of people view talk like this with skepticism.

Several years ago, the Great Lakes Indian Fish and Wildlife Commission did a big longitudinal study of bears, with cameras in bear dens across Michigan, Wisconsin, and Minnesota. They recorded birthing days and weather conditions. On the days the cubs were born, every time, the weather warmed up and there was a fog.

Scientists may be quick to point out that it was probably a shift in barometric pressure that brought on the fog and triggered a physiological response in the bears. My question is this: How did Nancy know? She didn't use the scientific method. But she knew. Ojibwe people have different and distinct bodies of knowledge and also different and distinct ways of knowing. And they are valid.

SEEKING SPIRITUAL HELP

There come times throughout our lives when we need spiritual help—someone to officiate a naming ceremony, a first kill feast, or a funeral. We benefit, too, from sustained relationships with spiritual mentors who can coach us on everything life throws our way. I have relied on my mentors in many ways, many times. I'm in my fifties at the time of this writing, and I still rely on my mentors, even though I officiate at many of the ceremonies mentioned here.

For those who seek mentor relationships or spiritual help from others, I recommend that you approach the effort in a spiritual way. Listen to your own spiritual instincts. Some years back, when many people were pointing out someone as the greatest medicine man ever, I felt uncomfortable around the person, and I later found out that he had some integrity issues. People nobody was pointing out have ended up being some of the most important mentors in my life. Each of us has a different personality. Some of us may need someone who is a true empath and can connect with us on an emotional level. Others may need someone who leads from their learned knowledge of a specific part of the cultural toolbox. What is right for one person may be wrong for another. And our needs may change over time.

There are a couple of red flags to watch out for when seeking mentors. First of all, if someone is charging money for ceremony or has a fee schedule for spiritual advice, it's probably a problem. Spiritual requests have a spiritual process. A lot of Ojibwe people have limited financial means. Those who perform spiritual service usually ask for tobacco and, for some ceremonies, food offerings or cloth gifts (such as a blanket). When I ask people to do a ceremony for me, I often give them some gas money as a way of saying thank you. But it's not a requirement. When I officiate for someone else, if they offer a monetary gift, I usually accept it, but I have never required money for my help. The other red flag to watch out for is compromised integrity. Spiritual mentorship is intimate. We share about our health needs and emotional pains. There needs to be trust for that, and it's a vulnerable connection. I always make sure spiritual advisors that I seek out or recommend don't have histories of violence or sexual misconduct. Weechi-it-te-win Family Services, which serves the Treaty Three area in Northwestern

Ontario, has a list of Ojibwe spiritual practitioners who have been vetted by a committee of culture carriers for knowledge of the language and culture and had criminal background checks. Mille Lacs employs culture carriers to advise people in the clinic on Ojibwe medicines and ceremonies, and they have been similarly vetted.

Good spiritual mentors keep healthy boundaries in their relationships with people they help. By helping people learn about themselves, acquire their spirit names, and go through ceremony or navigate grief and illness, spiritual mentors and their mentees can form strong friendships and deep mutual respect. Those healthy attachments can sometimes be confusing if there aren't good boundaries. Spiritual advising should not be confused with romantic attachment. Those seeking help can get hurt—and potentially be devastated to the point of stepping away from their cultural journey. And for the mentors, too, their integrity is a critical component of the service they provide to the people. Crossing that line in a mentor relationship is risky and ill-advised.

When you do decide to reach out, use tobacco. It opens doors spiritually, and it creates a spiritual connection that should help get a genuine spiritual response. If you are making a specific request (such as "What is my clan?"), I recommend asking one person rather than taking a survey of several culture keepers. If you ask seven people and get seven different answers, you'll have to ignore the directions of six of them and risk offending them. You'll also likely confuse yourself. Your integrity is best served if you stick to *your* teachings. And you'll best establish *your* teachings by starting with a primary guide. You can expand your web of relationships and mentors over time on your journey.

ONE ROAD

The Creator made a diversity of human beings on this planet. We speak seven thousand different languages, each just as beautiful as the next. We have many different cultures, and they are all beautiful in their own way. Some parts of these different cultures impact the others. In music and art, sometimes different cultures speak to one another in a way that transcends all of our socially constructed barriers. That's beautiful, too.

To live, though, is to walk one path. We can't walk two at the same time. While we can see and appreciate many cultures along that road, travel to many places, genuinely connect to many people, and to some degree even be multicultural, we have one road.

When it comes to religious choice and ceremony, we often have to make choices. In Ojibwe space it's taboo to mix and match two religious customs. At a funeral, we send the soul on one journey. I fully believe that there are many paths to the same place. We don't even have a concept of hell. We all go to the same place. But we can't send one soul on two different roads to that same place—it might get lost. So, we have to pick a path and walk it.

For me, I've followed my mother's road, Archie's road, the Red Road. My father, who was a Jew, was one of the most important people in my life. He celebrated Hanukkah, and we joined him. He came to sweat lodges and joined in. We shared deep understandings and appreciations. But for the kinds of ceremony that establish religious choice—a bar mitzvah, baptism and confirmation, initiation into our Ojibwe sacred societies, our funerals—we have to pick a path and stick with it. Our own spiritual development is best protected that way. And the clarity of direction makes it easiest for our family to support our path.

BEING MULTIRACIAL

In the Ojibwe culture, having just one Ojibwe ancestor is all it takes to open full-fledged access to the Ojibwe ceremonial world. Even so, a lot of us have been disconnected from that world. One-third of our babies have been adopted and fostered out of our communities. Over half of the enrolled citizens live off of reservations, and there's an even higher number of people who have Ojibwe ancestors but cannot be enrolled in a tribe because most tribes require proof of a certain percentage of blood from that particular tribe. The records are messed up and sometimes missing, and the whole concept of blood quantum is un-Indigenous and anti-Indigenous. None of those things make someone less than or unworthy. None should be a source of shame.

Lots of Ojibwe people are multitribal and multiracial. Some of us look black. Some of us look white. Some of us look brown. Some of us look racially ambiguous. Race itself is a social construct. It's not our way to out, marginalize, or exclude our fellow Ojibwe people from the circle because of the way they look.

Sometimes people can be cruel, and Native people are no exception. But trying to out-Indian one another or play identity police is really a sign of insecurity and is out of alignment with our core values. The cultural toolbox is full of healing, connecting, and positive identity-developing opportunities. These should be available to all Ojibwe people. My nine children cover a wide range of the color spectrum. My son Robert looks black; he has a big 1970s-style afro. My son Caleb and daughters Mia and Luella are much lighter and can pass as white or are assumed to be Latinx or Middle Eastern. Jordan, Madeline, Evan, Isaac, and Elias look more identifiably Native. I have them all stride into the powwow grounds, the ceremonial drum dance hall, and other ceremony spaces like they own the place. And they do. If you have Ojibwe heritage, it's your cultural toolbox, too. Don't worry about anyone else. Come join us.

NON-NATIVES AND THE OJIBWE CULTURAL TOOLBOX

I am heartened to see many non-Natives who have looked into the Ojibwe cultural toolbox and appreciate the beauty of our ways. I know from many deep conversations with my white wife and my white father that sometimes it's hard being white. It sounds funny to say that, considering racial dynamics in America that have so often privileged white folks. But it's true in a cultural sense. Often white folks who want to have genuine spiritual experiences get frustrated with the institutions that filter their religious and spiritual journeys. I have many friends who have the opposite experience, too—people of many racial backgrounds who find the rituals and guidance of the Catholic Church, for example, enable them to feel the hand of God. For those who feel frustrated and disconnected, it is easy to romanticize—and sometimes possible to find genuine appeal or affinity with—Ojibwe ways. It's understandable, but tricky. How are non-Ojibwe people to navigate Ojibwe boundaries around what's appropriate without appropriating a culture that is not theirs?

The answer, from my perspective, is all about listening to Ojibwe culture keepers. We know what's okay and what's not; we just need everyone else to listen and pay attention if the answer happens to be no. Archie had clear lines and guidance, and I now stick to his rule book in my roles as a culture keeper. Our sacred societies only initiate people who have Native ancestors. If we took everyone, there wouldn't even be room for the Ojibwe people, and if we took one, there would be no way to refuse anyone else.

Some parts of the culture have to be appreciated from a distance rather than owned by people who aren't Ojibwe. At the same time, our practices are kind and inclusive in many ways. We often take guests to observe ceremonial drum dances, participate actively in powwows, and engage directly in many cultural activities. When my kids had their first kill feasts, Blair held the spoon and offered the food to them. We need our whole families to understand and support our toolbox. And all of my kids are multiracial. I love every part of them, not just the Ojibwe parts. There is a oneness to all of humanity. We are all just pitiful humans trying to make our way in the world. Cultures are social constructs informed by spiritual realities that we filter through imperfect human lenses. Respecting our differences and seeing our oneness go hand in hand as we live and grow together.

NAVIGATING THE UNKNOWN

Humans have some big problems these days. Among those problems, race relations and climate change are especially daunting. I believe that the core values in our Ojibwe ways can provide powerful guidance. When we think and pray about what it means to respect all things and respect all beings, I believe we can find our way.

The spirits will keep giving to people. New people will receive new teachings, songs, medicines, and ceremonies. Cultures are changing all the time. New prophets may appear to help guide our endeavors and reconnect us to one another and to the spirits around us. While there are charlatans aplenty these days, there are legitimate voices, too. If we really listen, we will have help as we find our way.

CONCLUSION
Full Circle

Ojibwe people don't travel through the seasons linearly from spring to winter, from birth to death. We travel them in a circle. In winter, our connection to and reflection on the early phases of our lives deepen. In the circle, the end of a journey and its beginning touch one another.

At Princeton University I studied at the Woodrow Wilson School of Public and International Affairs with plans to follow in my mother's footsteps—to pursue a law degree, and maybe enter politics. I worked hard, and my studies went well; I found supportive teachers and made many friends. That world seemed ready to open to me.

I reached out to Paul Wellstone, Minnesota's firebrand US senator at the time. I felt like he was a liberal meteor streaking through the sky straight toward all the dinosaurs in Washington. He had won his first election to the Senate in 1990, the only challenger to defeat an incumbent that year—ousting Republican Rudy Boschwitz, who had outspent him seven to one. In 1991, I was trying to arrange an internship, and to my surprise, Wellstone wanted to meet me. It was my senior year in college. We met at Ruttger's resort in Bemidji, along with half a dozen staff members from his office. We chatted in the sun-soaked chairs by the lake. He was engaging, jovial, determined. He was short but strong, and he looked like the wrestler he had been in his younger years. He asked a lot of probing questions about education, race, and tribal sovereignty. It almost felt like he was baiting me to argue with him. I had no idea at the time, but he was actually testing my politics and my backbone. Wellstone served on the Senate Select Committee on Indian Affairs (now redesignated as the Senate Committee on Indian Affairs). At the end of our chat, he said that he didn't want me to intern in his office. He wanted to offer me a full-time job as his liaison on Indian affairs.

This was everything I had been building toward. It was a real opportunity and a chance to learn from one of the politicians I admired most. My ego was flattered by the offer, too. But I hesitated. He said, "You'll need to think about this. One of these guys will be in touch in a week or so." He nodded to one of his staffers.

This was exactly what I had wanted for years. But something had been shifting for me during my last couple of years at Princeton. My time away from the Ojibwe motherland had made me hungry for home. I knew I could be a good lawyer and maybe even a good politician. But I was losing faith that I'd be a happy one. And more than that, I wasn't so sure that it was my true calling. I wanted to live in Ojibwe country, to study my language and culture. I'd heard about a famous spiritual leader named Archie Mosay, and I wanted to see him. I had so many questions. But Wellstone seemed so certain. And a culture quest seemed so ethereal and untethered. It could wait.

I asked for advice from my parents. They smiled, but they did not tell me what to do. I think they were sure that I'd be on a plane to Washington as soon as I finished my senior year. There wasn't really another job or opportunity to compete with it. My mom told me to go down to the lake and put some tobacco in the water and I'd know.

I stood by the shore and watched my tobacco fan out on the surface. The red-winged blackbirds were trilling in the tall grass a few feet away. I weighed my decision, but somehow I knew this was a decision I couldn't make by logic alone. If the Great Spirit had a plan for me, I'd have to listen spiritually, not just intellectually. I told myself that if law and politics were meant to be, I'd have another opportunity someday. But getting in the woods to fast and getting to Archie for ceremony was more time sensitive. The old man wouldn't live forever. And how could I go through life *thinking* I knew what I was meant to do? I needed to *know*, and that meant a journey on the Red Road for me.

I was in motion as soon as I graduated from college. I went fasting and made my fateful journey to see Archie. I signed up for language classes and leaned in to building my cultural toolbox. I have no regrets. I love my life. Part of me wonders what would have happened had I taken the other fork in the road. Maybe I would have made my older dreams come true. Maybe I would have been sitting next to Paul, Sheila, and Marcia Wellstone when their plane crashed in 2002. Regardless of those unknowns, I do know now that I found my true calling.

Almost thirty years later, I had a profound sense of déjà vu as I watched my daughter Madeline wrestle with her career choices. I was developing a new relationship with my mother and my daughter at the same time. It was deep in the winter of my mother's life before I realized that my longing for my childhood days, when I had all of her time, was really a yearning to know that I simply had all of her heart. The revelation that I did gave me great comfort and enabled me to absorb her teachings about our ways and the love she bore for me in a way that I hadn't before.

The experience I had with my mother echoed for me with Madeline. She came into the world soon after I took the fork in the road that led me to Archie Mosay. In those days, I was a constant presence at drum ceremonies and other cultural events, and Madeline was always with me. Because we traveled the Red Road together, she had my wholehearted attention for the first four years of her life.

I chose to deepen my commitments to our ways, and with that choice came many blessings, but also new pressure on my time. And that pressure got harder to navigate when Madeline's mother and I parted ways. I soon had a new relationship and new children, too. Madeline went from having me to herself to sharing me with a family of several people and an Ojibwe universe full of people eager for my help. It was a cruel rearrangement of her world. I longed for the unpressured time I had with her for its own sake, but also because I feared that nothing else would communicate the depth of my love for her as effectively as my undivided time and attention. And my time and attention were always divided now.

Madeline proved remarkably resilient, though she, too, had scars and pain from the journey. Her story on the Red Road is a book in itself. By the time she finished college, Madeline had developed the ambition to help create an Indigenous birthing center, so Native women could be supported by their cultural toolbox as well as modern medicine. She was told several times that midwives and doulas would have no traction in the modern medical world, that only those with MDs could shape the rules and systems that deliver care. So, she developed a plan to go to medical school, get a PhD in a dual program, and build an Indigenous birthing center from scratch. Her resolve is incredible—but so, too, is her capability.

Madeline has clarity about her academic and career and cultural life. But tests from her childhood popped up as she prepared for her transition. I took her to my mom's house, and we smoked a pipe, prayed, and talked. We put down a bowl of food for the spirits. I shared with her the stories I've shared with you in this book. I told her that love is infinite. When a parent has more than one child, it might divide the parent's time, but it doesn't divide the love they hold for each child. I told her that I never could find a way to give her all my time again, after the rearrangement of our world when she was a child and its many rearrangements over the course of her life, but that she always had my infinite love. Things were better for both of us after that. I'm so grateful for the way that little ceremony and a lifetime of Red Road walking with our cultural toolbox has kept pulling us together.

Our ways are a road, and no two journeys are the same. My life choices are not a template for the rest of Ojibwe country. They are just one way that one man has walked the journey. The same can be said for Madeline's journey or anyone else's—whether the journey is in a city or on a reservation. The spirits find us wherever we are. The cultural toolbox has meaning and use for all who trek the Red Road.

We become what we do. How we spend our time matters. We need to feed the relationships and endeavors that define us, even though people don't need all our time to have our whole hearts, even though the most critical endeavors of our lives don't need all our time to have our wholehearted commitment. As I think about traditional living in the modern world, there are two important lessons I hope to leave for you here. For those walking the Red Road, don't beat yourself up if you can't walk it like our ancestors. We live in a different time, and it's not just acceptable or natural but *necessary* that we traverse the entire world we live in without shame. And secondly, our culture is not a place we go or a ceremony we do; it's a toolbox that we carry with us everywhere we go.

You are a complete, fully realized human being. You are a soul who has a body. You are the one your ancestors were praying for and waiting for through the generations. You have been given a unique set of gifts, and you yourself are a gift to the world.

Human beings have been through a lot. And we all need healing. Colonization has been brutal and dehumanizing to everyone. White folk were busy colonizing one another for a long time before they took it to the rest of the world. They need healing, too. Healing happens by decentering the colonial way of doing things. Each group of people on the planet has its own cultural toolbox. I encourage all of you, regardless of your race or cultural background, to lean in to yours. Decentering the colonization and starting the healing can happen in many different ways. For me, it happens every time I use my cultural toolbox. Learning our language is a powerful healing and decolonizing act. It decenters many forms of oppression. Our culture is identity, and our culture is healing.

We don't live in two worlds. We live in one world. We don't have to code-switch to make it out there. We don't have to maintain a dual consciousness. People from other cultures don't have to sacrifice theirs to enter our world, and Natives don't have to sacrifice their cultures to navigate the modern world. We can be exactly who we are—exactly who the Creator wanted us to be—and thrive. I'm an imperfect vessel, but this is how I do traditional living in the modern world. Giga-waabamin miinawaa.

APPENDIX 1
Bagese Rules

BAGESE, SOMETIMES CALLED the "bone dice game" in English, is a game for two to eight players of any age or gender. The bagese set comprises a wooden bowl, six to eight inches in diameter; one hundred cedar sticks; and eight bone or deer-antler figurines: one woman, one fish, two knives, and four small circles (sometimes called spots or buttons). The pieces are small, approximately one-half inch in diameter and one-eighth of an inch thick, and they're colored red on one side and white on the other. We have a special pillow for the bowl, although it can rest on any kind of cloth. We also have a bag to keep the set in.

Everyone has to pay to play—there is an ante. Commonly, people ante items of comparable value or agree on an amount of money.

Our bagese set. ***Anton Treuer***

We sometimes gamble chores with our kids; for example, everyone antes up half an hour of chore time. This is a winner-take-all game, so whoever wins can avoid cleaning or doing dishes for a month by claiming duties from everyone else in the house. Originally, Wenabozho played for the lives of Anishinaabeg against evil spirits.

To start, someone is appointed banker and holds the hundred cedar sticks. The qualifying round begins with each player, in clockwise direction, taking a turn shaking the bowl. The bone figurines flip around, and the player wins points according to how they land. A score is made when any figurine lands in the dish as the only figurine that is a different color from all the others.

woman = 50 points
fish = 20 points
one knife = 15 points
two knives = 30 points
one spot = 1 point
two spots = 2 points
three spots = 3 points
four spots = 4 points
all one color = 8 points

The woman scores when she is red and everything else is white, or when she is white and everything else is red. Players also score when any contrasting figurines are the same: if one knife is showing white and all the other pieces are showing red, it scores 15. If everything else is showing red, but two knives are showing white, the score is 30. The same goes with the spots: if anywhere from one to four spots show one color while everything else is the other, they score. If all pieces land showing red or all showing white, it scores eight sticks. In the qualifying round, a player who scores collects that number of sticks from the bank. The qualifying round ends when the bank is empty. If anyone got skunked during the qualifying round (no points), they pay the ante a second time and sit out the rest of the game.

The main game begins when all the sticks are distributed in the hands of all the players, based on their wins in the qualifying round. When someone makes a score in the main round, they collect the number of points from *each* player. A player who doesn't have enough sticks to cover gives what they do have, and then they are out of the game. If there are many players, people often start to get eliminated quickly. Play continues until there are only two players left.

When the game is down to two players, the sticks are reallocated. Each player gets twenty-five sticks; the others are put aside. The two play until one gets all the sticks. That player gets to take everything that has been anted up.

If at any time during any round (qualifying, main, or final) someone makes the figurine of the woman stand straight up, the game ends and that player collects all winnings, regardless of how sticks are distributed at the time.

APPENDIX 2
Ojibwe Taboos, Sayings, and Superstitions

THE OJIBWE HAVE TABOOS, sayings, and superstitions that range from the deeply spiritual to the comical. Some, like the metaphor of the ax, can be a motto or guidepost in life and others are pure amusement. Some are widely known and others less common but still part of the cultural tapestry. Tom Cain wrote a collection of stories, never published, called "Know Your Heritage," in which he lists some of the taboos, sayings, and superstitions I am sharing here. Others I picked up over the years from Archie Mosay, Tom Stillday, Anna Gibbs, Melvin Eagle, and other culture carriers.

1. If there is ever a bramble in your life, pick up your ax.
2. I hope you live so long that you can no longer crush a raspberry between your gums.

3. If you hear a buzzing sound in your ear, it could be the spirits of departed souls calling you to join them, so shout, “I’ll only leave when I can’t chew a raspberry anymore.”

4. If you have a scary dream, share it with someone to lessen its power.

5. If you dream of a relative dying, share the dream with them; it gives them life.

6. If you have a powerful good dream, keep it to yourself so you don’t dilute its power.

7. If you dream of a dead relative, send them a food offering.

8. Don’t tell legends out of season (when it’s not winter) or a giant toad will mark you with blue welts.

9. Don’t play with fire or you’ll wet the bed.

10. If you put your shoes on the wrong feet, you will meet your clan (animal, bird, or fish).

11. If your anus itches while you are away from your spouse, someone is trying to steal your mate.

12. If a snowshoe hare bites you, you’ll live a long life until your hair is as white as a snowshoe hare in winter.

13. Don’t whistle at night or the spirits of the dead might think you are calling them and they will call back to you to accompany them.

14. Children should not play outside at night as they might play with the souls of the departed.

15. Close the window curtains, drapes, or blinds at night or the souls of the departed might look at you.

16. If you drop your tobacco pouch or food falls off your plate onto the floor or the ground, the spirits are asking you for extra offerings.

17. Don’t point with your index finger: it is a challenge and may be considered rude.

18. Don't point at the sun with any finger other than the thumb or you might lose that finger later in life.

19. A boy should not play women's games or his penis will stop growing.

20. A girl should not play men's games or she will develop extra-large nipples and bags on her breasts.

21. If you accidentally use the wrong edge of a knife, throw it over your shoulder so your spouse doesn't pass away.

22. If you are dressing an animal and the hip joint squeals when you cut it, the dead animal is calling a live mate and you shall kill another soon.

23. Process the animals you harvest right away or they will tell their kin that you are killing them and you will be less successful on your next attempts to trap, snare, hunt, or fish.

24. If you don't offer the first berry you pick to the bears, you will have an experience with a bear soon.

25. If you kill two woodchucks on the same day during the winter, you will have an experience with a bear soon.

26. Don't put things you use on your head (combs, hats, bandanas, hair ties) on the floor or you will get headaches.

27. If an owl comes right up to your window and peers in, there will be a death in the family.

28. If there is a loud knock on the door at night but nobody is there, there was a death in the family or the area and the soul of the deceased was trying to visit.

29. If a star-nosed shrew comes into your house, kill it; it could be bad medicine.

30. If a dog speaks to you in a human language, kill it; it could be bad medicine.

31. Don't marry someone from your clan or your children will be infertile.

ACKNOWLEDGMENTS

WHILE I AM A PRODUCT OF PREVIOUS GENERATIONS, I am a product of my learned culture, too. For that, I need to acknowledge my parents—Margaret Treuer, who lived her culture and taught me all she could, and Robert Treuer, who supported that effort in ways that amplified my mental and spiritual health and knowledge. Archie Mosay was my greatest teacher, and I am honored, but humbled and sometimes terrified, to succeed him in some areas of his service to our people. I have learned from many, many others, including but not limited to Tom Stillday, Anna Gibbs, Dora Ammann, Betsy Schultz, Connie Rivard, Leonard and Mary Moose, Porky and Hartley White, Joseph Nayquonabe Sr., Melvin Eagle, Skip and Babette Sandman, Eugene Stillday, Dan, Dennis, and Nancy Jones, Sean Fahrlander, James Hardy, Charles Grolla,

Adrian Liberty, Giniwgiizhig, Dustin Burnette, and Keller Paap. My family remains my greatest motivation and my greatest support for everything I do with the cultural toolbox. Miigwech to my siblings, Megan, Micah, and David, Derek, Paul, and Smith; my children, Luella, Mia, Evan, Elias, Isaac, Caleb, Madeline, Robert, and Jordan; my grandchildren, Kendrick, Zendaya, and Ambria; and my wife, Blair.

ABOUT THE AUTHOR

Dr. Anton Treuer is professor of Ojibwe at Bemidji State University and author of many books. He is editor of the *Oshkaabewis Native Journal*, the only academic journal of the Ojibwe language. Treuer has presented all over the United States and Canada and in several foreign countries on Everything You Wanted to Know About Indians But Were Afraid to Ask, Cultural Competence & Equity, Strategies for Addressing the "Achievement" Gap, and Tribal Sovereignty, History, Language, and Culture. He has sat on many organizational boards and has received more than forty prestigious awards and fellowships, including from the American Philosophical Society, the National Endowment for the Humanities, the National Science Foundation, the MacArthur Foundation, the Bush Foundation, and the John Simon Guggenheim Foundation. His published works include *Everything You Wanted to Know About Indians But Were Afraid to Ask*, *The Language Warrior's Manifesto: How to Keep Our Languages Alive No Matter the Odds*, *Warrior Nation: A History of the Red Lake Ojibwe*, *Ojibwe in Minnesota*, *The Assassination of Hole in the Day*, *Atlas of Indian Nations*, *The Indian Wars: Battles, Bloodshed, and the Fight for Freedom on the American Frontier*, and *Awesiinyensag*. Treuer is on the governing board for the Minnesota Historical Society. In 2018, he was named Guardian of Culture and Lifeways and recipient of the Pathfinder Award by the Association of Tribal Archives, Libraries, and Museums.